star
style

"Style can be defined as the form of one's talent. For each talent a different style; but by talent I mean that interior virtue of spirit by which a man discovers for himself what he has not learned from others. A talent without individuality is not a real talent. And style means individuality, one's own way of thinking, feeling, expressing. In short, a person has style who has things of his own to say and knows how to say them in his own way, with a completely personal attitude and manner that does not necessarily have to be beautiful."

— Luigi Pirandello

star style

Hollywood legends as fashion icons By Patty Fox

ANGEL CITY PRESS

ANGEL CITY PRESS, INC.

Published by Angel City Press
2118 Wilshire Boulevard, Suite 880
Santa Monica, California 90403
310-395-9982

FIRST PUBLISHED IN 1995 BY ANGEL CITY PRESS

3 5 7 9 10 8 6 4

FIRST EDITION

ISBN 1-883318-03-3

Art direction and design: John Miller

LIBRARY OF CONGRESS CATALOGING-IN-PUBLICATION DATA

Fox, Patty
  Star style : Hollywood legends as fashion icons / by Patty Fox ; design by John Miller. — 1st ed.
    p. cm.
  Includes bibliographical references and index.
  ISBN 1-883318-03-3 (hardcover)
    1. Motion picture actors and actresses—California—Los Angeles—Costume. 2. Fashion—History—20th century. 3. Costume—History—20th century I. Title.
  PN1998.2. F68 1995
  791.43'026'0979494—dc20 95-32222
            CIP

For Paddy Calistro, my treasured friend, whose commitment to this book made it reality.

Contents

trODuCtIoN

When actress Cybill Shepherd wore high-top tennis shoes to a televised awards ceremony in 1985, she planted the seeds of *Star Style*. One couldn't help but wonder why some stars are fashion icons and others just solitary entries in a Hollywood book of memorable moments.

In the glamour years of Hollywood — a period that stretched from the 1920s to the mid 1960s — no self-respecting goddess would have met her public in orange sneakers and a black velvet gown. Elegant, chic, sophisticated, glamorous, unique and oh-so-carefully orchestrated — these words describe Hollywood's legendary pacesetters. To be indiscriminate, haphazardly thrown together or trapped in the current "hip" uniform is the affliction of a modern Hollywood in search of its style. The icons knew better. In those glamorous days, stars dressed for the audiences, taught their audiences by example, showed those audiences the possibilities. The stars and their adoring fans shared the fantasy of fashion.

Only a handful of actresses have left an indelible image embedded in the collective mind of the world. Fewer still have become legends of style whose personal flair is integrally linked to their stardom. Swanson, Del Rio, Dietrich, Garbo, Day, Katharine and Audrey Hepburn, Ball, Crawford and Monroe knew how to dress to captivate both men and women. These celebrities rarely listened to the studio bosses when it came to shaping their own images; they didn't compromise; they knew how to make an impact. Unwilling to lose control,

they collaborated with studio designers, sometimes actually sketching clothing ideas and selecting fabrics and accessories. Both on and off the screen these leading ladies had the guts to be different, to create looks that would be copied for decades and, perhaps, forever.

The 10 trendsetters who developed in the glamour era were as diverse as their fans. Marlene Dietrich and Doris Day at first may seem out of place in the same book. Yet their impact on an adulating public was the same — their devotees dressed like them, watched for their new takes on fashion, tracked the evolution of their wardrobes. Greta Garbo and Marilyn Monroe took opposite approaches to dressing — one covered up and the other uncovered — yet both enticed their audiences with an enduring sex appeal. Two clotheshorses, Gloria Swanson and Dolores Del Rio, succeeded in the same Hollywood, one a poor girl from Chicago who never felt pretty, the other a born beauty from Mexico whose privileged life let her focus on her own loveliness. How much more different could Joan Crawford and Lucille Ball be

when it came to clothes? Crawford wore the power clothes of a '40s career girl, and lovable Lucy played the harried housewife with a bandanna on her head. Yet both shaped styles that made their fans want to go shopping. The diversity of Hollywood's fashion legends offered something for everyone. Each star succeeded in attracting a huge audience that related not just to the clothes, but also to the sense of self those clothes projected.

As Edith Head once acknowledged: "Glamour and having a consistent look means something to the public." Stars of the '20s, '30s, '40s and '50s rarely strayed from their carefully shaped images. Today, without the studio system to direct them, female leads turn their glamour on and off. Try as she might, Madonna hasn't qualified as a fashion legend — not yet, anyway. Her look is too erratic and derivative: a little Marilyn Monroe, a little Jean Harlow, with some Jane Fonda as Barbarella thrown in. When she finds her *self* in her clothes, her hair, her makeup, she'll be in the running. But compared to a Katharine Hepburn, who routinely defied fashion, or an Audrey Hepburn, who constantly defined it, a celebrity

rowed from the designers. Or maybe we secretly resent the idea that if we're willing to splurge, we too can go to Saks Fifth Avenue or Neiman Marcus (for the real thing) or The Limited or J.C. Penney

who re-creates style history doesn't shape it.

Designers worked with their stars to establish and reinforce their images in the days when the studios knew that a star's fashion appeal equated with box-office bonanza. Today fashion designers look back to old Hollywood for inspiration. Armani's carefully tailored suits look to be borrowed from Dietrich. Isaac Mizrahi once claimed that Lucille Ball was his muse. And Calvin Klein calls Kate Hepburn the inspiration for America's casual chic. As if to come full circle, today's well-dressed stars turn to these well-known ready-to-wear designers to clothe them off-screen. They look beautiful, sometimes even ravishing, but something's missing. Call it mystery. Maybe the problem lies in the fact that we know the clothes we see our idols wearing on Academy Award night are bor-

(for a copy). Maybe we simply want our stars' looks to be out of our reach. An Armani-clad Jodie Foster or a Donna Karaned Barbra Streisand is doubtlessly glamorous, yet lacks the *je ne sais quoi* of days gone by. In Garbo's day fans wrote letters begging to buy just one of her Adrian gowns at any price, but, alas, they weren't for sale. Fans still rush to clothing auctions when a glamour queen passes on — even a single piece of a celebrated wardrobe is worth fighting for.

Maybe the current stars haven't mastered the lesson from watching their chic predecessors, but we can. The 10 fashion profiles that follow reveal the leading ladies' elements of style, the image how-tos of Hollywood's high priestesses. But their stories do more than that — they prove that these women took control of their images and created their own success. Therein lies the importance of understanding star style for them and, perhaps, for all of us.

GloriA Swanson

Sunset Boulevard's melodramatic and grandiose style with its flamboyant visuals and that kitschy Old Hollywood glamour was pure Gloria Swanson. No one — neither Mae West nor Pola Negri, who were also considered to play the famed Norma Desmond — could have captured the essence of the silent screen era the way Swanson did. Film's first full-fledged "glamour girl," a five-foot-one-inch dame who never finished high school, was a maestro of creative visualization. Dressing as lavishly off-screen as her mentor Cecil B. DeMille costumed her for his movies, she used clothes and attention-grabbing gestures to bolster her confidence and her image. And it worked. Making a grand entrance draped in her finery, she *became* the tall, dramatic intellectual she always wanted to be.

In a thriving new industry where women were always seen and rarely heard, Swanson was an anomaly. She was the first actress to turn down a million-dollar studio contract because she knew she was worth more. She collected and cast away husbands the way movie moguls bought and sold hot properties. She was even gutsy enough to have a baby at the peak of her career. By 1926 she had opted into co-ownership of United Artists, and by 1933 people were calling her a has-been. When she died, they were calling her a legend.

But in 1915, the teenager from Chicago didn't seem to have a lot to offer Hollywood. An army brat whose parents had just divorced, she wasn't well educated or schooled in drama. Even she knew she wasn't a looker. A shrimp in high heels, her waist was too thick and her ears were too big.

Undaunted, young Gloria Swanson was determined to crack the film capital. Early on, her mother taught her little Glory to use clothes to accent the positive, to camouflage the negative and, above all, to make a statement. Mom had encouraged her to never copy what the other girls wore, to feel special for being different. The maternal advice paid off.

Wearing a distinctive black-and-white checked skirt with a green waistcoat and cropped black jacket, the would-be actress caught the eye of a casting director. He eventually got her a part as an extra in a Charlie Chaplin flick. When she auditioned for Mack Sennett, who was hiring bathing beauties for his popular slapstick comedies, she convinced the producer/director that she was a comedienne and he hired her for *A Dash of Courage* (1916).

Though she dressed well and often wore her personal wardrobe in those early films, it wasn't until she went to work for Cecil B. DeMille, in *Don't Change Your Husband* (1919), that Swanson became a world-famous clotheshorse. DeMille turned her into a box-office magnet for fashion-starved females. Dripping with diamonds, furs and the sexy silks and satins that DeMille lavished on his stars, the petite actress became a huge and glamorous presence on the screen. Outside the studios her entrances became grander and grander as she donned ermine coats and hats heavy with peacock feathers. She always entered carrying her trademark, a single red carnation.

As extravagant as DeMille, Swanson relished the idea of Pinkerton guards coming to her dressing room bearing treasure chests

"When I am a star, I will be every inch and every moment a star."

— Gloria Swanson

Swanson tucked pink silk roses in the neckline
of her favorite gown, opposite, to blend with the
pink satin trim, drawing attention to the face. This
page, bands of art deco diamond links ring Swanson's
upper arm as she applies lip color from the diamond-
studded case of her own design in *What a Widow* (1930).
To play up the sparkle, her gown is edged in rhinestones.

"I was one of a kind."
— Gloria Swanson

Swanson's playful nature and desire for one-of-a-kind costumes are showcased in her Mack Sennett film, *A Pullman Bride* (1917), her final picture for Sennett. "The world of slapstick was not for me — I felt it was just not respectable. I hated the vulgarity that was just under the surface of it every minute." Opposite, costume designer René Hubert consults with a fur-suited Swanson.

filled with jewels from which she could accessorize her next costume change. Once, after having been frightened by hungry lions in an elaborate scene, the leading lady actually sat on the producer/director's knee as he attempted to soothe her. Though the stellar attention might have been enough for most adult actresses, Swanson wasn't totally assuaged until DeMille offered her a brilliant trinket. "I picked out a gold-mesh evening purse with an emerald clasp and immediately felt much better," she recalled.

She did six consecutive films with De-Mille, in which she was clad in his flashy costumes. Despite her preference for the lavish, she was astute enough to recognize the difference between Hollywood screen glamour and good taste. Trips to New York and Paris were educational. By astute observation, she taught herself how to dress. The artistry of fashion appealed to her aesthetic sense, and, like a painter, she began to formulate the look that would be Swanson. She was such a big draw that even the opinionated DeMille allowed her to lead when it came to fashion.

The new, more sophisticated look showed up first in *The Humming Bird* (1924) and *Manhandled* (1924). After those two films, she over-

hauled her personal wardrobe. She nixed the sugary pastels that Mary Pickford had popularized as well as the fantasy gowns sprinkled with silver stars she herself had worn in the early DeMille films. Swanson's new look featured expensively tailored, monochromatic ensembles that elongated the illusion of her short body. In a surprising twist for a petite woman, she favored oversized hats, bags and jewelry. She disguised her short neck with enormous cowls and wore turbans and bandeaux to minimize the appearance of what she deemed an overly large head. She replaced the elaborate and very artificial updos that DeMille preferred with chic, sleek hairstyles she felt were more befitting an international celebrity.

Soon her strong facial characteristics, the very features she tried to hide, were symbols of American glamour. Freed to look like herself rather than studio moguls' old-fashioned image of beauty, Swanson's new style opened the door to new definitions of allure. She was always uncomfortable being called "pretty" or "glamorous," preferring "handsome." Now she not only had to adjust to being a benchmark for beauty but also a role model for women who felt shortchanged in the looks

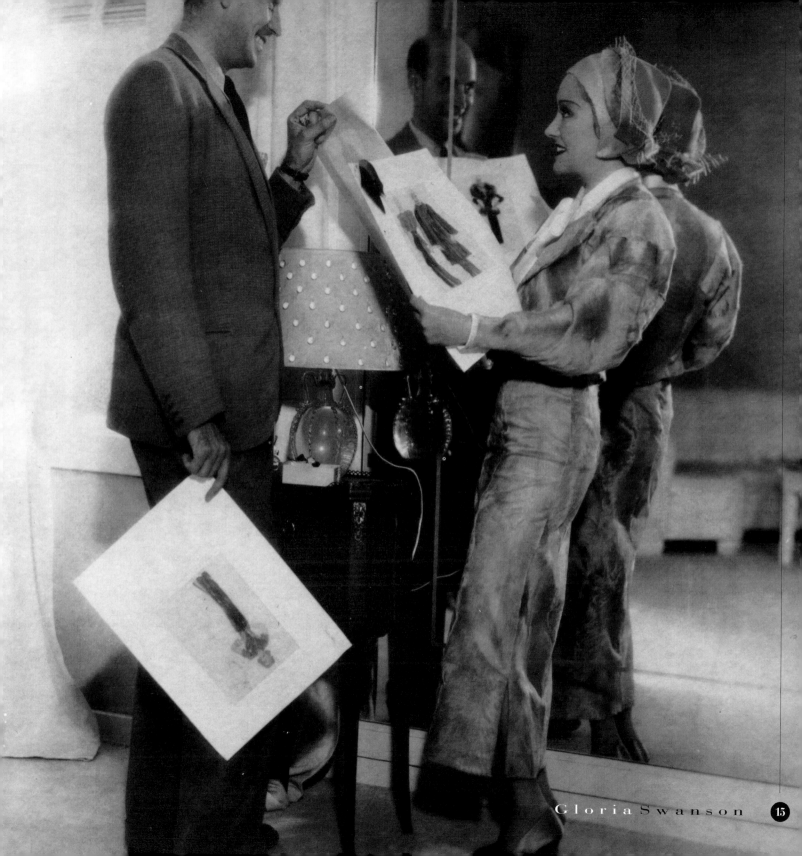

"Don't give me anything dinky," cautioned Swanson. The oversized adornments she wore off-screen, this page and adjacent, were more "movie star" than her costumes such as the simple black dress and pearl lariat, far right, in *Queen Kelly* (1928) .

"The public wanted us to live like kings and queens, so we did."

— Gloria Swanson

category. Although women with prominent mouths began flaunting their Swanson-like smiles, the star owned up to hating her teeth. "They were so big and square that I always kept my mouth covered with my hand when I smiled." Long after the press was calling her smile "dazzling," she referred to her "horse teeth" and "tombstones."

One of the first stars to film a movie in the foreign location where the story was actually set, Swanson spent months in France making *Madame Sans-Gêne* (1925). While she was there, she absorbed every visual lesson ("Always watch what the shopgirls wear in Paris — they have the most style," she taught her daughter Gloria), and she continued to refine her image. At the time her wardrobe included some 300 dresses and suits, 100 pairs of shoes, and enough hats to fill five long shelves (to vary the look of those hats, she kept a large supply of trims on hand). She rented a beautiful townhouse (she felt cramped at the Crillon Hotel), had a Rolls-Royce in robin's-egg blue (with her chauffeur and footman dressed to match it), and set about establishing her-self in French society. One sure method was to marry a titled Frenchman. She accomplished that shortly after meeting the Marquis Le Bailly de la Falaise de la Coudraye. That marriage ended in divorce, following the pattern of her others, the first to the actor Wallace Beery and then to Herbert Somborn, who owned Hollywood's famed Brown Derby. She would have six marriages in all, including those to Michael Farmer, William Davey and Bill Dufty.

Her return to the States with her French husband in 1925 was perhaps her most momentous entrance. She reportedly sent a wire to DeMille noting, "Am arriving with the marquis tomorrow, please arrange ovation." Designer Edith Head recalled being called away from her wardrobe studio to join a small throng tossing roses at the newlyweds. It was an appropriate welcome, for not only did Swanson bring back the marquis, a new film and a *tres chic* wardrobe, but she had knocked Mary Pickford out of the catbird seat as America's favorite actress. Swanson was the biggest female star in the world.

"She walks with an air of a woman glamorous" — Edith Head

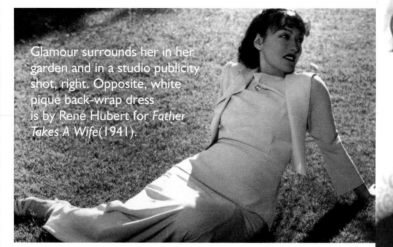

Glamour surrounds her in her garden and in a studio publicity shot, right. Opposite, white piqué back-wrap dress is by Rene Hubert for *Father Takes A Wife* (1941).

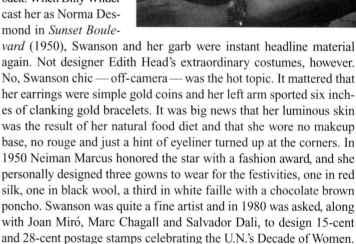

Swanson paired diamond-encrusted crystal bracelets for day and evening outings. A cowled hood, secured with a diamond brooch, extends the white-column gown for a maximum illusion of height.

Spending $50,000 for gowns, $9,000 for stockings and $6,000 on perfume in the 1920s was no easy feat, but this woman knew no limits. She spent what she made, all in the name of living up to her legend. But in 1929, her star crashed with the stock market. Everything associated with luxe living lost its luster, including Swanson. "If there's one thing harder to be than being a celebrity, it's being a has-been," she told the *Los Angeles Times.* "So you have to go right on, especially since you must raise a family and support them."

She left California in 1938. She once explained that she was through with Hollywood because Hollywood was through with her. She filled the periods between her various "returns to the screens," by indulging her many interests. A natural food aficionado since 1928, she invested in a natural cosmetics company and international pollution research in the '50s. She even worked as a reporter for United Press International.

She could never resist a dramatic comeback. When Billy Wilder cast her as Norma Desmond in *Sunset Boulevard* (1950), Swanson and her garb were instant headline material again. Not designer Edith Head's extraordinary costumes, however. No, Swanson chic — off-camera — was the hot topic. It mattered that her earrings were simple gold coins and her left arm sported six inches of clanking gold bracelets. It was big news that her luminous skin was the result of her natural food diet and that she wore no makeup base, no rouge and just a hint of eyeliner turned up at the corners. In 1950 Neiman Marcus honored the star with a fashion award, and she personally designed three gowns to wear for the festivities, one in red silk, one in black wool, a third in white faille with a chocolate brown poncho. Swanson was quite a fine artist and in 1980 was asked, along with Joan Miró, Marc Chagall and Salvador Dali, to design 15-cent and 28-cent postage stamps celebrating the U.N.'s Decade of Women.

She died in 1983, with a career's worth of entrance-making clothing still jamming three storage rooms in her New York apartment building. The world's fascination with this tiny woman's dramatic image has endured. Shortly after her death, an auction raised $100,000 from fans anxious for one last memento of Hollywood's first "glamour girl."

who knows she's

JoAn Crawford

MGM's queen of shoulder pads was Hollywood's most obsessive fashion addict during the golden years. Joan Crawford literally *loved* every piece in her many closets and regarded the garments as her most intimate pals, buddies who would help her career and enhance her life. "I feel as if clothes are people," she once admitted. "When I buy a dress, or buy the fabric to have one made, that's a new friend. Am I to let it hang there and not give it warmth and affection? 'Course not!"

If *obsessive* sounds like too strong a word to describe her clothing addiction, consider the facts: She changed outfits as often as 10 times a day (sometimes even hourly), traveled with upwards of 35 suitcases, and carried several diamond necklace and earring sets in their own wardrobe trunk. A regular on the world's best-dressed lists, at one point she owned 16 fur coats, including ermines, minks, beavers and broadtail lambs. ("I look at them and I know that I'm a star," she would beam.) When she found the perfect hat, she had it copied in 12 colors. She wore falsies even when lying down, to be certain that her breasts pointed skyward. Known as a drinker, she swigged in style — she carried her 100-proof vodka in hip flasks with specially designed covers that matched her outfits. When guests came to her home, she led tours of her many closets: one each for dresses, for suits, for hats, for shoes and even one for handbags. There, her "friends" hung swathed in plastic. Fabric-covered shoes that matched each ensemble, her fashion trademark, were permanently sheltered in clear plastic, à la '50s sofas, to keep them spotless.

She may have needed her "friends" to cover up her insecurities. While playing the role of the star "Joan Crawford," she was, as some observers have suggested, plagued by the fact that she was still Lucille LeSueur, born on the wrong side of the tracks in San Antonio. Her eyes popped, her lips were thin, her mouth small, her brows wild. She knew her figure wasn't great. Short and squat at 5'4", she had size-12 hips and huge shoulders that provided her only real contours. To look like a star, she needed padding and a variety of Max Factor's paint to reconfigure her form and face for the camera. "I photographed better than I actually looked," she conceded, "So I tried desperately to make sure my makeup and wardrobe lived up to the image on the screen."

In 1925, a rather nondescript 21-year-old who bordered on pudginess, came to Hollywood, danced her way into a chorus line and eventually into a film called *Our Dancing Daughters* (1928), which was a box-office hit. By 1930 she had graduated to leading lady with an MGM contract and acclamation as "the perfect camera beauty," looking every bit the statuesque movie star.

It helped, of course, that she married Douglas Fairbanks Jr., in 1929, since his father's stardom made Junior the reigning prince of Hollywood. But Crawford had another essential ally in her journey to superstardom. From 1929 to 1943 the stellar designer Adrian created almost everything the actress wore both on- and off-screen. Until he streamlined her style, the ex-hoofer wore gaudy dresses with buttons, bows and frills. And because he found a way to turn

"Any actress being well-groomed is digging her

Only the balloon tires on the roadster date this photo of Crawford wearing trousers — her ensemble and shades look modern. The rare photographer captured Crawford in pants; here she's arriving at the studio for an early morning call. Her signature shoulder pads are as integral to the actress's image as her dark brow and lips and those faux lashes, opposite, in *Above Suspicion* (1943).

who appears in public without own grave."

— Joan Crawford

"Bags and shoes are my weakness. knitting is my avocation."

— Joan Crawford

MGM's Irene turns hundreds of metallic strands into feminine armor on a shapely dressmaker suit. Opposite, former hoofers get addicted to beautiful shoes and Crawford was no exception. Her footwear obsession was legendary, so the studio publicity department decided to play it up.

what he called her "Johnny Weissmuller" shoulders into a fashion trend, she worshiped him and the elegant image he created for her. In those days, "more money was spent on my wardrobe, per movie, than on the script," she recalled. "The image had to be protected."

Crawford was convinced that what she wore equated with her box-office appeal, so she adhered to her designer's every suggestion. In Adrian's hands Crawford became an overnight fashion sensation. Women who didn't read *Vogue* and *Harper's Bazaar* — and that was the majority of fashion-conscious women in the '30s and '40s — flocked to the theaters or devoured movie magazines to see what she and Adrian's other mannequin, Greta Garbo, were wearing. Draping Garbo in the slinkiest silks and Crawford in his most outrageous fabric architecture, Adrian developed his own adoring fans while

the actresses blazed in his glorious creations. When Crawford's big moneymaker *Letty Lynton* (1932) made its debut, Macy's immediately sold 500,000 copies of her white gown with organdy ruffles at the shoulders (which looks like a precursor to some of those good-witch gowns Adrian dreamed up for 1939's *The Wizard of Oz*). From 1933 through 1945, the Crawford look dominated fashion in stores from Saks Fifth Avenue to J.C. Penney. World War II fabric shortages reined in film designers' extravagant use of European silks and satins but not their creativity. Throughout the war women continued to go to the movies to fulfill their fashion dreams as well as their romantic ones.

Her shoulder pads left a lasting imprint on the history of fashion. Born out of the necessity to make

Chewing gum is my vice and

When Crawford lost this diamond brooch in a New York restaurant, the unsuspecting waiter who found it obviously determined that nothing *that* spectacular could be real, so he threw it away. Rescued from the trash, the sparkler remained one of her prized possessions, a personal symbol of her stardom. Her MGM film costumes and studio publicity shots, opposite, were consistent with the style of the clothes she wore off-screen. Only at far right does she appear with her unpadded, natural shoulder line, in a vivid green duster worn over an off-white gown from her personal wardrobe.

"She had a special outfit for answering the fan mail"

— Joe Mankiewicz

her already wide shoulders broader than her large hips, the pads became part of a fashion trend that lasted for 10 years and have been revived intermittently ever since. Adrian added the extra padding because, as he explained to her, "we can't cut 'em off, so we'll make them wider." Although the rest of the world looked at the style as a fashion trend, director Michael Curtiz was sick of her powerhouse shoulders by the time she auditioned for her Academy Award-winning role in *Mildred Pierce* (1945). As she recalled, "He looked at me and snarled, 'You and your damned shoulder pads!' reached out in fury, and ripped my dress from neck to hemline. Then he stared in shocked amazement. The shoulders were still there. They were real."

Crawford's presence was totally manufactured by the men in her early Hollywood days — Fairbanks, Franchot Tone and Adrian. She gained sophistication when she became part of the Hollywood elite with Fairbanks (whom she divorced in 1933) and later after she mar-

ried the very continental Tone. Before they split in 1939, he introduced her to the worlds of literature and fine art and taught her to appreciate fine food and wine. Her aesthetic judgment having improved, she began to hone her fashion sense. Though she experimented with her look over the years, she never had the confidence to personalize it and put aside the image Adrian had created. As Louella Parsons noted in the '60s when Crawford was still wearing shoulder pads and overdone makeup, "After playing Joan Crawford for 40 years, it's doubtful whether there is any private personality left."

Psychologists might suggest that her obsession with clothes reflected her need to take control of some part of herself. Perhaps. But when it came to analyzing what to wear when and to taking charge of one's wardrobe, Crawford had dressing down to a formula. The five fashion rules that she lived by were so important that she outlined them in her autobiography: "1. Find your own style and have the courage to stick to it. 2. Choose your clothes for your way

The eye has it in this publicity shot from *Grand Hotel* (1932).
Note the pale brow, with only a hint of rounded arch.
Opposite, Crawford's trademark turban brings full attention to
her face, especially when lit with a glittering diamond brooch.

"Joan Crawford was notorious for her falsies."

— Diana Dors

of life. 3. Make your wardrobe as versatile as an actress. It should be able to play many roles. 4. Find your happiest colors — the ones that make you feel good. 5. Care for your clothes, like the good friends they are!" When making public appearances, Crawford always wore bright colors, "to give them something to look at." For romantic interludes, she wore few accessories, advising others to follow her lead: "Underdress for a romantic scene, let your face and figure and your expression play the leading roles." Packing for a trip meant several hours of work, making sure that every garment fit, that each ensemble was complete with hat, gloves and accessories, and that dual-purpose clothes such as reversible coats and cocktail dresses with short and long interchangeable skirts were included.

She tried to be all things to all people, her friend Helen Hayes lamented after Crawford's death, "I just wish she hadn't tried to be a mother."

Columnist Sidney Skolsky summed up Crawford best in a 1947 article in the *Hollywood Citizen News:* "She is probably the only actress in movies who acts like a movie actress off the screen. She has never been caught with her makeup off or her slacks on." At least not in public. At home, Crawford dared show another side, as daughter Christina pointed out in the bestseller *Mommie Dearest.* Behind closed doors Crawford wore tasteless cheap cotton shifts, rubber sandals and not a speck of makeup.

On the outside, she was the complete star, dressed to the hilt. "I love being a celebrity," Crawford admitted. "I never go out on the street unless I expect and anticipate and hope and pray that I'll be recognized. That someone'll ask for my autograph! When they do, I'm prepared and ready and as well-dressed as I possibly can be. And when somebody says, 'There's Joan Crawford,' I say, 'It sure is!'"

Dolores
Del Rio

"God either gives you a face or He doesn't."

— Dolores Del Rio

Hollywood called her the female Rudolph Valentino, the Latina lover. The dark-eyed, raven-haired Dolores Del Rio, with her perfect face and sleek, exotic style, was arguably the most beautiful woman ever to work in Hollywood. Men found her irresistible. Producers and directors took one look at her face and gave her the lead. Even Orson Welles fell head over heels with the aristocratic actress from Mexico.

Thanks to her looks she was a box-office draw and sought-after leading lady. She was so stunning that it was difficult for directors to cast her in films opposite other actresses because she dominated any scene. And she was so exquisite and such a renowned mannequin for spectacular clothes that she quickly became known as a fashion icon in Hollywood, not as a great actress.

Hers was a legend built on her beauty and style. Dolores married MGM art director Cedric Gibbons in 1930, just after she'd become a huge hit in three silent films, *What Price Glory?* (1926), *Resurrection* (1927) and *Ramona* (1928), and had finished her first talking feature, *The Bad One* (1930). Their mutual obsession with the visual side of cinema overtook their life. Mr. and Mrs. Gibbons matched each other's elegance, he in his natty suits, she in her sophisticated gowns. Their home, a dramatic art deco manse in Santa Monica Canyon, was the perfect backdrop for a glamorous lifestyle filled with parties, stars and moguls. Dolores soon realized, however, that "Hollywood has a way of grabbing you and wrapping you up." She was distressed to discover that "when [producers] give you wonderful clothes, they give you bad parts." Yet she was addicted to being fashionable and could not fight her desire to look ravishing.

An exotic and sophisticated style like hers was unknown in the film capital when she arrived in 1925. Unlike the other "most beautiful women" in town — Mary Astor, Marion Davies, and Mae Murray among them — Dolores wasn't a fluffy, bon-bon type done up in ruffles and pastels. She had her own very personal style. Everything about Del Rio was sleek, from her lean body and the sculpted angles of her face to her long black hair. Her clothing, equally sleek, oozed chic simplicity, each gown fitting as if it were made for her, as indeed all of them were. Dolores's wardrobe was built on two basic neutrals. "I belong to the traditional French school of wearing black as the most elegant," she explained, "but white suits me best; it's good for my eyes and hair." Off-camera she was frequently dressed totally in white to set off her dark features, accented with her own diamond earrings or flowers from her garden. She often combined black and white in bold graphic blocks, stripes or

Del Rio collected diamonds from her earliest days in Mexico, so she had the trappings of stardom by the time she arrived in Hollywood. She wears her art-deco diamond brooch and bracelets in tandem as she chats with David Selznick, opposite.

Adding a Mexican flair to her silk charmeuse gown, a cape of dramatic fringe encircles Dolores's shoulders. Note the diamond bracelet, this time worn between bands of round beads. Opposite, avant-garde accessories make the difference here: metallic mesh gloves and a high-style hat that demands a beautiful face.

"Her exquisite, expressive face won her a wide following." — *Newsweek*

sophisticated florals, never the boring little frock prints that her contemporaries were wearing. Before she married Gibbons, film costume designers tried to Americanize her style, but Dolores persisted in bringing her cultural sensibility to her professional and personal wardrobe. In publicity photographs, she looked very avant-garde, with accessories worn in a way that reflected her Mexican roots: clusters of bracelets that covered both arms from wrist to elbow, or several necklaces layered over each other, or shoulder-grazing diamond earrings, fringed silk shawls draped over her shoulders, or cabbage-rose corsages bursting from her décolleté. By 1930, Adrian, who also dressed Crawford and Garbo, was designing for Del Rio and consulting with her about style.

Her intense eyes, her dramatic mouth and the defined planes of her face inspired the look of the '30s, though the trend was often attributed to Joan Crawford. Crawford's style, however, came long after Hollywood makeup artists had taken note of Del Rio in the '20s — arched, full brows and lids darkened with eyeshadows and black pencil, cheekbones accented with rouge, brown foundation used to "sculpt" the hollows, and full red lips.

The Latin star's compelling elegance was bred in her earliest years. Her family's elite social standing in Mexico forced her to learn the elements of propriety and high culture at an early age. With that came an understanding of style. Born in Durango in 1905, Dolores Asunsolo Lopez Negrette was the only child in one of her country's wealthy families, so she grew up like a princess, with a fine education in a convent school taught by French nuns. Her talent as a singer and dancer was

Dolores relaxes on a Santa Monica beach near her home, dressed in color-blocked linen and a matching skullcap.

as a woman has twinkles in her
no man notices whether
she has wrinkles under them."

— Dolores Del Rio

"She was the most beautiful woman I had ever seen."

— Orson Welles

cultivated in Spain and France, where she was taught by masters, and at the same time, she observed the cosmopolitan fashion world first hand. At 15 Lolita, as she was nicknamed, married Jaime del Rio, a man 18 years older than she, who accompanied her to the United States after she was discovered by a Hollywood producer, Edwin Carewe.

Rather than portray her as the typical "poor girl makes good" starlet to whom fans could vicariously relate, Carewe gambled by releasing publicity that focussed on her almost regal social standing. Fans heard about her meetings with the king and queen of Spain, her personal collection of diamonds and her European wardrobe. Her name quickly hit the list of "Hollywood's Best Dressed Women" and just as quickly became a must at every "A" party.

In January 1926 Joan Crawford, Mary Astor, Janet Gaynor, Fay Wray and Dolores were honored by the Western Association of Motion Picture Advertisers at an industry ball celebrating a total of 13 young women who were judged to "have shown the most talent and promise of eventual stardom." When the breathtaking young señora took the stage, following the other WAMPAS "baby stars," a hush fell over the audience of 3,500. Fearing she had been rejected, Dolores turned to leave just as the stunned crowd broke into a wild,

standing ovation that lasted more than five minutes. People wanted a longer view of this new aristocratic goddess — they had never seen anyone as beautiful. From that evening on, the exotic Mexican's career flourished.

As her star rose, her first marriage fell apart; her husband died and she soon landed in Gibbons' arms. He restyled and homogenized her image, downplaying her Mexican heritage. She cut her hair, abandoning her traditionally Mexican center-parted hairdo in favor of fashionable side-parted curly styles, and selected styles like the other Hollywood stars wore. But her beauty continued to set her apart. Her roles got progressively worse, but her clothes kept getting better. She found that she was relying on her clotheshorse image to sustain her career. When she was cast in *Flying Down to Rio* in 1933, she pulled strings to help now-renowned costume designer Irene get one of her first jobs. The musical was also the debut of an unknown dance team, Fred Astaire and Ginger Rogers, who got rave reviews. Though they stole the show, Dolores for the first time received kudos as a talented actress *and* introduced the two-piece bathing suit to the American cinema. Then came *Madame DuBarry* (1934), a talkie remake of the 1919 silent film with French period costumes worthy of Versailles. The same year *Photoplay* magazine called Del Rio the sec-

One of Hollywood's best-dressed women, when she dressed for special occasions, her favorite color was white, which complemented her dark hair and eyes. Her diamond bracelets, opposite, are worn paired as cuffs with a draped halter-neck gown. Even the collar is encrusted with real diamonds.

While married to
MGM art director
Cedric Gibbons, Dolores
socialized with moguls and
executives who would be
decision-makers in her
career. The parties in their
Santa Monica home were
renowned for their
elegance and extravagance.
Ready to set sail, opposite,
Del Rio paid as much
attention to detail as any
costume designer; every
accessory reflects the
two-tone color scheme
of her daytime dress.

"Every bad deed, every bad fault will show on your face."
— Dolores Del Rio

ond most beautiful woman in Hollywood, with Garbo topping the list. Studios fought to sign the dark-haired actress. By 1940 she had been under contract to United Artists, RKO, Warner Bros., Columbia and 20th Century-Fox.

Her notorious love affair with Orson Welles occurred shortly after she divorced Gibbons in January 1941. Caught in the controversy over *Citizen Kane* (1941), Welles needed distraction and found her. "I used to follow her around — at a discreet distance, of course — just to admire her," the 26-year-old producer-director-writer said just before casting her in *Journey into Fear* (1942). But the film fizzled and the fickle boy wonder of Hollywood met his soon-to-be-wife, Rita Hayworth. Heartbroken, and with a career on the wane, Dolores packed up her gowns and returned to Mexico in 1943.

In her homeland, she became the queen of the cinema. She demanded important scripts and took charge of her wardrobe, so she had everything she wanted. At one point she reported that she had 400 Parisian-designed gowns, 250 pairs of shoes, "so many furs that I've lost count" and 200 bottles of perfume in her dressing room at home. Shunning American style, she again adopted Mexican accessories such as heavy silver jewelry and rebozos as part of her everyday attire. The most celebrated actress in Mexico in the '40s and '50s, she won four Ariels, though she had never come close to winning its United States counter-

part, the Academy Award (which, incidentally, ex-husband Gibbons had designed). As she matured, she occasionally returned to Hollywood to make films such as *Flaming Star* (1960), in which she played Elvis Presley's mother, and John Huston's *Cheyenne Autumn* (1964). By then her favorite personal designer was Oscar de la Renta, who covered her in sequins and beads to flaunt her still-perfect figure.

In her heyday, on- or off-screen, Del Rio balked at wearing trousers, except perhaps to do the gardening at home. A paparazzo caught her clad in a silk pajama ensemble cha-chaing with Errol Flynn at the nightclub La Conga shortly after her marriage to Gibbons broke up in '41, but pants were a rarity. She was the ultra-feminine type, almost always dressed in suits or dresses, hose and heels.

Dolores Del Rio had built her career on being more beautiful than most mortals, even the Hollywood kind. She resisted exercise, preferring massages to stimulate her circulation and sleeping sometimes as many as 16 hours a day to maintain her beauty. Before she died in 1983, she summed up her secrets, "God had given me whatever beauty I may have had, and I took care of it in good health. I don't smoke or drink. I eat conservatively. I walk and swim. I clean my face thoroughly at night with a good, simple cream and cold water. . . . The only sign of age I see is that I am becoming an institution."

Greta Garbo

The moment she came to Hollywood, circa 1925, the Swedish Sphinx pulled on her slouched hat, turned up the collar of her trench coat and veiled herself in mystery. With that, Greta Garbo became the world's most enigmatic screen star. Like no other actress, she used her clothes to hide from her public. Yet the more she covered up, the more her understated, quiet style entranced her audiences, enhanced her mysterious image and turned her into a perennial symbol of chic.

A perfectionist whose self-image didn't match the public's perception of her, Garbo didn't like the way she looked. Although she wasn't particularly tall at 5'7" or overweight at 126 pounds, she felt she was too big and gawky, so she dieted constantly. She believed that her neck was too thick, and her hair was relentlessly fine and frizzy. Her first leading man, Ricardo Cortez, reinforced her insecurities, deeming her "not especially beautiful." Directors complained that Louis B. Mayer had made a mistake in importing a foreign leading lady with a flat chest, thick legs and a less-than-feminine image at a time when the public preferred the petite-doll personas of Mary Pickford and Norma Shearer.

Born Greta Louisa Gustafson in Sweden in 1905, Garbo the actress obsessed on her self-described flaws, then set about making the most of what she had. She would never be tiny and curvaceous, but she had a body that could look elegantly long and lean, an appealing form in the late '20s. Attempting to obscure her "faults" or create more pleasant optical illusions on-screen, Garbo inadvertently shaped the foundation of her signature fashion look: pants and long gowns for a lean line, very high necklines and, of course, hats that covered her hair, revealing only that face.

Critics may have denigrated her body, but Garbo's face was flawless. Modern-day plastic surgeons have cited it as the benchmark of perfection, noting that its dimensions are in consummate balance: the lower lip only slightly fuller than her shapely upper lip, eyes well spaced with one eye's width between them and at each temple, the nose length exactly one-third the distance from hairline to chin. Less analytical types simply would say that with her long, thick lashes, her finely chiseled features and her pearlescent skin, she was a looker. Off-screen she needed only a modicum of makeup, just a touch of eyebrow pencil, a light lipstick, a dusting of powder and a lavish coat of mascara on her long, naturally pale lashes. That face helped to convince Mayer that she was worth the $18,200 contract he had waiting for her when she arrived from Stockholm. At a time when Joan Crawford was lucky to be making $75 a week, a five-figure salary meant that Garbo came to the American cinema already a star, however unproven.

As extraordinary as her face was, Garbo's personal wardrobe was common. "I care nothing about clothes . . . When I am off the set, I don't want to have to think of clothes at all . . . I like to live simply, dress simply." Comfort was her priority. At times her need to be comfortable interfered with her image, as Joe Ruttenberg, a Hollywood photographer of her day, commented, "Unfortunately, she had a taste for bulky, ugly clothes that made her look much older than she was.

"An enigma in the form of a goddess. . ."

— *Newsweek*

It was like she couldn't stand to look beautiful, she only felt comfortable frumpy." While "ugly" is a subjective term, there's no arguing that the Swede opted for practical styles that sidestepped the current vogue.

Desperate to find shoes that didn't hurt her feet, she bought hundreds of pairs — but rarely anything pretty. Instead of elegant, feminine high-heeled shoes that would showcase her surprisingly delicate size 7AA foot, she opted for oxfords and loafers. The choice caused such observers as Hedda Hopper to spread the word that her feet were big. Actor David Niven tried to clear up the matter, noting that Garbo's feet were "actually gracefully shaped and well proportioned for her body type" but she had an unfortunate habit of encasing them in huge brown loafers that gave the impression that she wore "landing craft." On the set when her feet didn't show in the frame, Garbo wore furry bedroom slippers and constantly asked the cameraman, "Is the feets in?"

Her less-than-dainty shoes actually complemented her clothes. "Town and country" tweed skirts and trousers, oversize coats, suits, cardigan sweaters and turtlenecks were her uniform. The first woman to popularize a turtleneck (previously, it was strictly jockey's garb), she chose it for strictly practical reasons. The high-necked sweater was not only comfortable, but it also slimmed the appear-

ance of her neck and called attention to her face. Once she discovered its advantages, she developed several variations on the style: scarves wrapped and tied at the neckline, collars that were buttoned or tied high and tight. She found ways to adapt the turtleneck for day or evening, so she never had to be seen in a low-necked gown. Though her reasons were strictly pragmatic, her fans glommed onto the look, and the turtleneck became a classic.

Her signature trench coat had equally practical roots: She loved walking in the rain. The mannish style suited her — she ordered coats long enough to skim her calves or ankles, depending on the season, and the cut worked with many fabrics. She could wear a trench coat over her bulkiest sweaters and jackets, yet cinched in at the waist, it still gave her a semblance of curves. It could even do double duty, as on the night she went to Chasen's, a Los Angeles restaurant whose dress code forbade pants — she simply rolled up her trousers and hid them under her coat. Perhaps most important, for Garbo a coat was a perfect way to create mystery. Outsiders couldn't learn any more about her than she offered.

A hat model at a department store in her native land, the young Greta had a hat on her head when she stepped off the boat from Stockholm, and it seemed that she never took it off. Her fans didn't care that she was hiding her hair — they liked the effect. Studio pub-

The diagonal white collar, opposite, shapes a
slimming illusion for Garbo, who felt "too big"
in the earliest days of her career. The flower on
the shoulder draws attention to her face.
Known for her hats, Garbo rarely selected an
attention-grabbing shape like this oversized
portrait style.

"The real Garbo
screen Garbo could not"

— *New York Times*

Photographer Cecil Beaton described his beloved Garbo as "The moon-coloured enigma, the femme fatale with the Chinese-black eyeliner above the fantail lashes." She emphasized the shape of her eyes with dark shadows defining the hollow under the brow bone. Her makeup was consistant both for day and evening.

could afford to grow old; the

"I wish I could be
mysterious like her."

— Marlene Dietrich

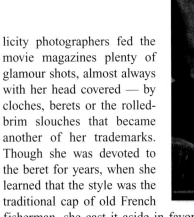

licity photographers fed the movie magazines plenty of glamour shots, almost always with her head covered — by cloches, berets or the rolled-brim slouches that became another of her trademarks. Though she was devoted to the beret for years, when she learned that the style was the traditional cap of old French fisherman, she cast it aside in favor of something more feminine. Although everything she wore below the neck may have been practical and slightly masculine, her hats were an extension of her face — they had to be beautiful. Unlike those of other stars of the day, however, her hats depended far more on their architecture than their trims for their effect. The purpose of her headgear was to flatter, not detract from, her face.

By the time she made her second film, *The Temptress* (1926), Garbo's screen career was set. Critics hailed her as "svelte of figure" (Mordaunt Hall, *New York Times*) and "a delight to the eyes! . . . She leaves nothing to be desired" (Harriette Underhill, *New York Herald Tribune*). But she had yet to establish her image in costumes. Her seventh film, *Woman of Affairs* (1929), was assigned to designer Adrian Adolph Greenberg, who would make her his muse. After viewing the

mishmash of gowns that were hung on her in the first six films, Adrian recognized that her personal style had more to offer than anything she had worn on-screen. He designed ensembles for her that could make a sometimes blah movie worthwhile. In *A Woman of Affairs* she looks chic in a bulky wool trench coat over a high-necked blouse, slouched hat and flat shoes. He adapted the trench to a silk evening gown and kept almost every neckline higher than that worn by any other star of her day, except perhaps little Shirley Temple. Draped cowls, stand-away collars, shallow V-necks and very high jewel necklines became the Garbo/Adrian signature.

America responded. Garbo became the hottest trendsetter in the country. Her fans all over were covering up instead of baring. Mascara sales skyrocketed, and faux lashes became a rage. The streets began to fill with Mata Haris hidden under trench coats. She and Adrian were a hit. Eventually, however, director George Cukor tired of her style and instructed the designer and her hairdresser, Sydney Guilaroff, to give her a new look for *Two-Faced Woman* (1941). The results were

With her town and country sweater and skirt, Garbo wears the sensible, comfortable shoes that launched an inaccurate but persistent rumor — that she had big feet. Ferragamo, who made more than 70 pair of shoes for her, confirms that she wore a 7AA, actually a small foot for her 5'7" frame. In one of the few smiling shots, opposite far left, of the mysterious Garbo, she topped her trousers with her favorite coat look, a modified trench style that helped camouflage flaws only she perceived. Note that she selected an unusually feminine ankle-laced ballet slipper. Comfort was always her priority. Left, sedate touches of gold lamé trim were Garbo's concession to dressing up. Her elfin slippers were as close to going barefoot as the Swedish star could find.

Wearing a sophisticated variation on her signature turtleneck, Garbo selected this dress with an asymetrical rolled collar. Her hair was cut to peek perfectly underneath the famed slouch hat she holds here. On the set of *The Single Standard* (1929), right, Garbo gives a rare glimpse of her athletic legs. Garbo lost control of her look in *Two-Faced Woman* (1941), far right. At director George Cukor's bidding, Sydney Guilaroff cut and permed her hair. Adrian added frou-frou to her once understated garb, the only touch of her old elegance being scattered diamond clips. The fans rejected Garbo's much heralded "new look," however. She starred in no more films and Adrian resigned from MGM after the release of this film.

"When the glamour ends for Garbo, it ends for me."

— Adrian

disastrous, starting with the low-cut dresses Cukor demanded and ending with the old-lady hairdo Guilaroff cut and permed into shape. *Time* called the effect "almost as shocking as seeing your mother drunk," and the *New York Times* pinpointed her "appallingly unflattering clothes and makeup."

Two-Faced Woman was not only her last film, but also Adrian's. He tried his hand at a designer boutique but failed. Garbo turned herself over to Valentina, the New York couturière. They had been introduced by Garbo's beau, Gaylord Hauser, the millionaire nutritionist who guided her digestive life and was one of a string of homosexual boyfriends (a list that included the great photographer Cecil Beaton). Garbo became infatuated with Valentina and her husband, George Schlee, and the trio seemingly developed a *ménage à trois*. The women often dressed alike, Valentina calling herself "the Gothic version of Garbo." Valentina instructed Garbo to "fit the century, forget the year," advice that left the star undistracted by seasonal fashion trends. The Russian dressmaker limited the color range of Garbo's wardrobe to white, ivory, beige, navy and black and eschewed prints or patterns of any kind. Though Valentina adhered to Garbo's strict rules of design, she interpreted them in a new way. The results were loose and easy shapes that provided more variety than Adrian had ever given her. In fact, Garbo once demoralized the man who had worked with her to create her image by absolving herself of responsibility and telling him, "I never really liked most of the clothes you made me wear."

Garbo appreciated Valentina's ability to translate her look into a softer yet more sophisticated style. Adrian's approach had become predictable — a terrible fate in Garbo's mind. Such was her need for privacy, she didn't want anyone to be able to categorize her style. Just when her public thought they understood her, she found a new take on her look. Valentina, Monsieur X, Lanvin's Castillo or Balenciaga — the interpreters were always of the highest fashion caliber.

The Swedish Sphinx never gave up her trench coat, be it wool, nylon, faille or taffeta. And she never gave up her slouch hat. For more coverage, she added sunglasses. These accessories were not just her signatures, they were integral to her aura of mystery. No one will ever know if she planned that image or just slipped into it — comfortably.

Marlene Dietrich

As she explored the cabaret district of Berlin in the late 1920s, Marlene Dietrich concluded that only transvestites knew how to sport a garter. She especially admired one blond drag queen who wore a white satin top hat. That, she decreed, was style. And so it was that a German silent-screen actress decided she was woman enough to dress like a man and become a star. Indeed, decked out in tails, Dietrich seduced the world.

First, however, she captivated Josef von Sternberg, the director who spotted her on stage in Berlin in 1929 when she, pushing 30, was still a bit player. Dazzled by this totally sensual vision whose legs were more appealing than any of the cleavage he'd seen in Hollywood, von Sternberg urged her to put her androgynous image on the screen and became her Svengali, working with her on her next seven films. He introduced her to American audiences as the heartless heartbreaker Lola Lola, wearing a top hat in *The Blue Angel* (1930). Next she followed him back to Paramount Studios for *Morocco* (1930) where, clad in her own tux, she kissed another woman and catapulted to stardom.

She refused to wear tails in her next two films. An unusual combination of strategist and artist, the glamorous new star knew that such gimmicks were good for getting noticed, but otherwise extremely short-lived. For *Blonde Venus* (1932), she agreed when von Sternberg insisted on a scene with white tails and top hat, but afterward Dietrich went tuxless for decades. Still, the image-obsessed actress was clever enough to analyze her renowned boy-girl look and understand why it worked. On a psychological level, wearing blatantly man-tailored clothes appealed to subliminal urges in both men and women in her audience (urges that she, a bisexual, had no problem understanding). On a purely visual level, menswear on a woman, especially this woman, was incredibly sensual. It was those legs, bared or covered by trousers. The legs were her instant sex appeal.

Dietrich's shrewd analysis established that there was a brain behind her image, hers. By uncovering the two critical aspects of her image that would become her lasting trademarks — wearing menswear styles and focussing attention on her legs — she pinpointed the essence of what was to become her legend. Indeed, her legs and her propensity for pants would change the course of women's fashion.

They were legs no longer than many (after all, Dietrich was only 5'6") and in no better proportion than many others in Hollywood. But they were legs that she made *appear* extraordinary. She always, for instance, wore shoes that minimized her feet (which she hated) and added the illusion of length to her legs. At a loss to find the right foot covering in retail stores, Dietrich had most pairs custom-made, patiently enduring hours of meticulous fittings. "Shoes are more important than suits and dresses. Good shoes give elegance to your entire appearance. Buy one pair of good shoes instead of three pairs of bad quality," she said. She also nixed vibrantly colored footwear

Dietrich often chose leathers for her personal wardrobe, left. Here she flies in black and white. The bare-shoulder gown from 1934, above, was a fore-runner to Donna Karan's "cold-shoulder" gown worn in the White House by Hillary Rodham Clinton in 1993. Opposite, Dietrich brought attention to her legs with lace-appliqued hosiery, in *The Devil Is a Woman* (1935).

"I always did want to get into Dietrich's pants."

— Tallulah Bankhead

in favor of black, brown or navy shoes, each worn with matching hosiery, noting, "Your legs look longer when the color of your shoes doesn't act like a stop sign." Dietrich often wore two-toned shoes on- and off-screen. She went so far as to claim that Coco Chanel had copied the actress's design when the French couturière marketed the light shoe with the dark toe cap, another way to make the leg look longer and the foot shorter.

It took more than glorious shoes to make those gams world famous, however. Just before *Morocco* opened nationally, the Paramount publicity machine plastered cities with billboards that showed Marlene and her bare limbs, the first time that Hollywood had actually showcased an actress's extremities. She and her Paramount studio designer, Travis Banton, worked tirelessly to create costumes that celebrated those shapely legs. For *The Devil Is a Woman* (1935), she convinced Banton to abandon the bare-legged look typical of a Spanish dancer and decorate her legs with

lace-encrusted stockings. For *Kismet* (1944), Dietrich actually risked her health by painting her legs with gold metallic paint, which sealed her pores and caused her to collapse on the set. But those notorious legs did shine in the film and despite the wartime battles that the newspapers chronicled, her brush with lead poisoning made the front pages. Dietrich favored skirts with strategically placed slits that allowed her gams to be bared now, covered then. During the war, when she entertained troops wearing a sequined-and-slitted gown, she played a carpenter's saw with a bow. She positioned her body the way a musician might play a cello, but her "instrument" was held tightly between her legs — the stunt was something only a woman as bold as Dietrich could pull off. She wore yet another gown with a slit on Academy Awards night in 1951. She received a standing ovation after strutting across the stage to present the Oscar for Best Foreign Film, an entrance she had carefully planned to allow the best view of a single exposed leg.

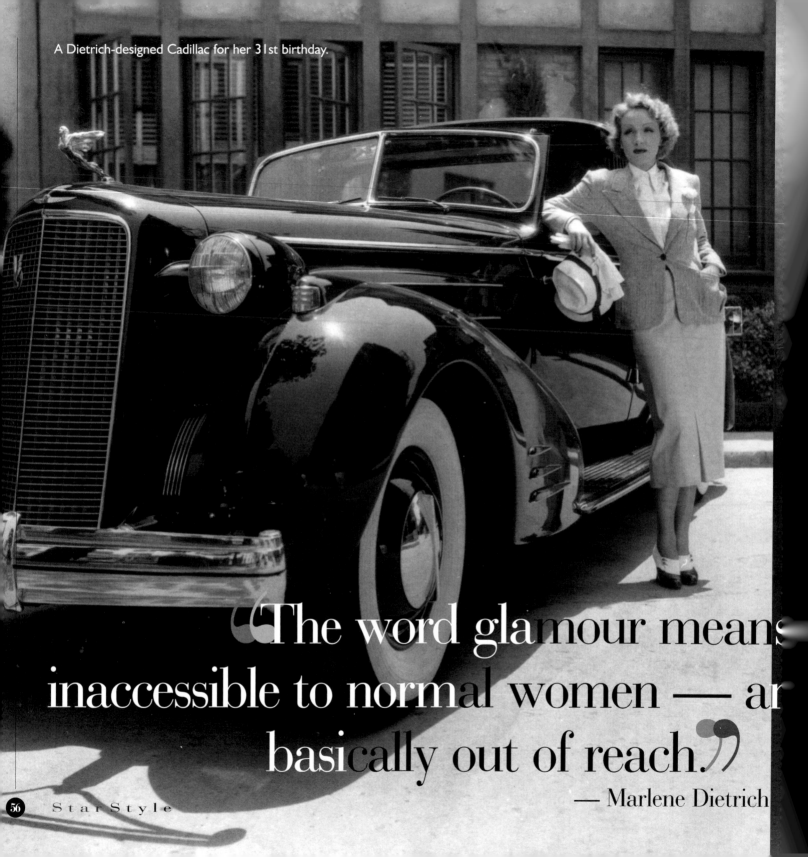

A Dietrich-designed Cadillac for her 31st birthday.

"The word glamour means inaccessible to normal women — and basically out of reach."

— Marlene Dietrich

Von Sternberg and Dietrich both interpret menswear for evening.

All in the attitude, the tilted hat, the gloves, the nonchalant gaze.

something indefinite, something
unreal paradise, desirable but

"Hitler had wanted me as his mistress. Maybe, if I had consented, I could have saved the lives of millions of Jews," Dietrich said after World War II. She often told stories of how the German dictator had tried to woo her back to Berlin. Instead, she called entertaining American troops "my finest hour." Opposite, Dietrich brought so much drama to her personal wardrobe that Paramount used her clothes in publicity shots.

"She's not content with being merely beautiful."

— Noel Coward

As Dietrich aged, she never deviated from her leggy image. When her limbs began to suffer from circulation problems, she designed tall boots to cover swelling. As the problem persisted, she kept an array of sizes to accommodate the various stages of puffiness and the bulk of the bandages. Because she couldn't anticipate the degree of swelling, she often traveled with eight sizes of the same boot in various colors and patterns.

Though she never flaunted the rest of her body as flagrantly as she showed off her gams, Dietrich tended to it carefully. Her breasts posed the most confounding problem. They drooped visibly, a catastrophe when body-hugging clothes were the style. She purchased hundreds of brassieres over her lifetime, trying to find the perfect support for breasts that she repeatedly called "ugly." After the war, when silk was available again, Dietrich invented her own total body girdle to shape a flawless form under slinky, often near-trans-parent gowns. Constructed of silk souffle from Italy, this contraption was strong enough to mold her figure, yet sheer enough to go unnoticed under her most gossamer gowns. The tight garment was under so much pressure, it often burst as she wore it. To be ready for such emergencies, she kept three dozen extras on hand while filming. The result of the torture of merely climbing into and adjusting her body parts to fit this weightless armor was a perfect form, something she always desired. Torture for beauty was integral to Dietrich's Prussian ethic; success was worth the suffering.

In the early 1960s she tried to convince her audience that her shapeless bosom was "in," noting, "Today's fad requires large, soft, hanging breasts that can be easily displaced." Yet she persisted with her pursuit of the perfect bra. At home, out of the public eye, she went braless, hiding her figure flaw under oversized men's silk pajamas.

"All her life Marlene was wearing a mask."

— Maximillian Schell

Ever the Star and ever aware of her image, how she clothed her body was of utmost importance. The early lesson about the subliminally sexual appeal of women dressed in menswear caused her to assert her independence at a critical time in history. When Dietrich came to Hollywood, Depression-repressed female moviegoers wore frocks printed with nosegays and equated sex appeal with the chesty look of Mae West. This new siren bucked the trend by baring her fabulous legs and covering her bosom. Perhaps even more revolutionary, this woman, who didn't like her own breasts, caused the world to shift its focus from above a woman's waist to below. She often wore slacks to cover those gams, but as a veil of mystery. The pants turned the waist, hips and derriere into sexual enticements, freshly outlined zones that would drive men wild. While with the USO entertaining World War II troops at the front — part of her personal quest to defeat Hitler, which earned her the American government's prestigious Medal of Freedom — she wore regulation Army trousers, proving to each soldier just how sexy it could be to have a woman in his pants. Dietrich's war effort gave Rosie the Riveter the

Von Sternberg used shadows from Venetian blinds to replicate the diagonal lines of Dietrich's veil in *Shanghai Express* (1932), far left. Her man-tailored flair for travel, center. After the war, her Army ribbon becomes a tiny jewel on her shoulder.

unspoken permission to dress like a man while she worked like one. Unintentionally liberating women's dressing traditions forever, Dietrich had her own pantsuits custom-made by her husband's tailor, found ways to wear trousers for both casual and glamorous events and showed the world that it wasn't necessary to display a calf or the turn of an ankle to make legs looks sexy.

Dietrich never believed she had a beautiful face. Good bones, perhaps, but she would never admit to being a beauty. She was no egotist. Obsessed with her appearance, yes. Self-centered, yes. But not an egomaniac. She objectified herself, treating her beauty as her power and as a tool to accomplish her career goals. She obsessively kept that tool honed to perfection. The highest paid woman in the world in 1936, Dietrich's determination to be unforgettable

Dietrich followed von Sternberg's technique throughout her career, always lighting her face from above to carve severe angles. She found ways to distract attention from her hands, which she usually tried to conceal, by using dramatic diamonds over gloves and a cigarette holder, right, or her own diamond-encrusted platinum cuff with a cabochon emerald and mammoth ring, top left.

Marlene Dietrich

Dietrich entertained troops playing a saw, a talent she acquired in 1927. Body-hugging gowns required a sheer, high-necked foundation so tight that it shaped the famous body. She used diamond jewelry, right, to conceal it at the neckline. Each bauble on this gown designed by Jean-Louis, opposite, was adjusted to create the perfect illusion for her grand entrances.

"I have never

on the screen made her a star even when some of her films flopped.

A friend of hers once said that Dietrich "was beautiful because she wanted to be beautiful." The strength of her determination affected not just the way she felt but how others viewed her. She did have a few makeup tricks that helped enhance her looks, however. To style the perfect face for her role in *The Devil Is a Woman*, for instance, the actress plucked out her brows and pencilled on a higher, thinner, more dramatic pair, setting a 1930s trend that many women still haven't abandoned. To keep her mouth muscles taut, she sucked on lemon wedges before every close-up in every film. To camouflage the pudgy digits she despised, Dietrich girdled her hands in custom-fitted gloves that were so tight she couldn't bend her fingers. When she couldn't wear gloves, she made certain her hands were either hidden in pockets or gracefully wielding a cigarette holder in a cloud of smoke. Dietrich was so skilled at applying makeup and styling her hair, that she was the only star ever to be admitted as an honorary member of the film makeup and hairdressers' union. To be certain her nose always looked its best, she blended a pale stripe of foundation down its center, for a slimming, straightening and lengthening effect. To make her eyes look their biggest and brightest, she used a hairpin to apply white liner on the pink shelf of her lower lid (never black liner under the eye because it minimized the illusion of great size). The movie magazines of the day claimed that she dusted her hair with pure gold to make it shimmer. The false rumor was believable because she sprinkled golden

mixed privacy with my profession."

— Marlene Dietrich

powder in her reddish blonde hair to make it appear paler and perhaps, even more so, because von Sternberg artfully used overhead lighting to make her tresses glisten.

When she began to perceive minor sags in her face, she turned to master hairdresser Sydney Guilaroff for a surgery-free facelift, though it may have been as painful as the knife. Guilaroff made dozens of minuscule braids from wisps of hair along her hairline, twisting, pulling and securing them until her scalp bled, her teeth throbbed and her face was pulled taut. Hair naturally stretches, so the magic would last just until lunch hour, when Guilaroff would be summoned back to start pulling again.

Dietrich approached her image with total passion. She was obsessed with being the perfect woman to please her public. That essential image extended way beyond the screen to every aspect of her life. Every nuance of her existence had to be just as she envisioned perfection to be (that even included her notorious slew of lovers). "In life," as she called those private hours away from her craft, she had exactly one husband (indeed, the same man, Rudolf Sieber, for 40 years, despite her many lovers, both male and female) and exactly one child (a daughter, Maria,

born in 1925, who grew up under her mother's tutelage to be the perfect assistant and Hollywood handmaiden). She cooked, she cleaned, she nurtured. All part of the actress's fantasy image of the perfect wife and mother. She lived it.

Dietrich was her own creation. On-screen or off, wherever a camera might click, every detail of her appearance and her life was meticulously orchestrated. She shaped her own stardom, her own style, her own impact on the world. She blamed other women for their own mediocrity. Most of them, she complained, "must have the assurance of others — they must have the seal of approval to be sure they haven't made a mistake. But that is where they make their mistake." When it came to her own image, Dietrich made no errors. Never a follower, she knew her formula, she relied on it, and approval followed her.

Katharine Hepburn

In 1928 a professional voice coach instructed 21-year-old Katharine Hepburn to stop dressing like a scarecrow, "throw away that old felt hat and get one without a hole in it."

"What's the matter with people?" the fledgling actress retorted. "Can't their imaginations supply enough cloth for that little hole?"

Throughout her century-spanning career, the singular star has thumbed her nose at attempts to conventionalize her image and demanded complete acceptance for her iconoclastic style, eccentricities and her fanatic need to be comfortable.

Her independence was not always rewarded. Just about the same time Marlene Dietrich became an overnight sensation in trousers, Kate Hepburn donned men's pants and took a licking for it. But Dietrich wore pants to turn her legs into erogenous zones; Hepburn preferred trousers because she wouldn't tolerate wearing stockings with garters and couldn't abide short skirts. Dietrich oozed appeal while Hepburn reeked of arrogance. Marlene became a box-office smash, while Kate struggled, bombing on Broadway. Like Dietrich, however, Hepburn wasn't about to fail. Nor would she change her style to succeed. Indeed, she would use it as a means to her end.

"I bet it takes us longer to look as if we hadn't made any effort than it does someone else to come in beautifully dressed," the independent actress once said to Greta Garbo. While Hepburn pretended that she didn't care about clothes, she knew that her eccentric, put-together style was perfectly studied. Dietrich and Garbo opted to borrow chic from the well-suited gent. Hepburn chose to look as though she had simply taken her father's hand-me-downs — slouchy sweaters, oversized pants and scruffy loafers.

Born the eldest daughter of a doctor and a suffragette, Kate learned early to suffer the slings and arrows that come with being an independent thinker. Her dad championed increased education about venereal disease while her mother helped women get the vote, then supported birth control. Both were activists who gave controversial speeches and used public venues to advance human rights causes. Most of the community dismissed the Hepburns as offbeat kooks. Some openly shunned them. Such treatment only increased her parents' resolve. Their daughter absorbed the childhood lesson that being unique was an honorable distinction, a way to stand out from the crowd. Since her parents ultimately achieved their revolutionary philosophical goals by fearlessly risking public censure, she came to view nonconformity as a positive attribute.

Determined to attract attention, Kate started wearing pants at a very early age. When she was eight, she wanted nothing more than to be a boy, so she buzzed her red hair into a crew cut, dubbed herself Jimmy and wore dungarees whenever possible. During her college years at Bryn Mawr, she tried wearing flared skirts with matching sweaters and felt "painfully self-conscious." But in her drama classes there, clad in trousers, she played leading men with ease (except once, that is, when she put her hand in her pants pocket, sat down and then couldn't extricate the hand).

Just after her senior year ended and eager to clinch her first acting

"How can I do a
under her fingernails
and

Hepburn and Tracy
consult between takes on
the set of their films. Her vest
and pants are all boy, on a break
during *Guess Who's Coming to
Dinner* (1967). Opposite, she
covers newspaper curlers with a
bandanna and rides a bike while
filming *Woman of the Year* (1942).
Preceding page, in a portrait from
Holiday (1938), Hepburn wears her
simple makeup and sleek cap of
waves, offset by a trio of
coordinated diamond strands
and a starburst brooch.

picture with a woman who has dirt always wears pants?""

— Spencer Tracy

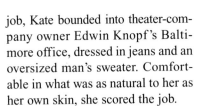

job, Kate bounded into theater-company owner Edwin Knopf's Baltimore office, dressed in jeans and an oversized man's sweater. Comfortable in what was as natural to her as her own skin, she scored the job.

Pants were still her uniform when she was a leading player at RKO. Desperate for a glamour girl, studio executives threatened that if she didn't stop wearing dungarees they would steal them. She didn't and they did. She retaliated by announcing, "Unless you give me back my pants I intend to walk through the RKO lot naked." When she stepped out of her dressing room in nothing but silk underpants, the studio heads, fearing the worst, capitulated and returned her jeans.

Now, at eighty-something, she continues to wear pants, looking quite like a magazine advertisement for one of those stores whose marketing message is that khakis know no bounds of age, class or protocol.

Hepburn was outfitted with diamonds in her films throughout the

years, but the accessory she wore most often off-camera was the utilitarian safety pin. References recur to her strategic usage of the tool, some dating back as early as 1928 when, in Mrs. Robinson-Duff's voice class, the eager student would sport a man's sweater secured at the back with one. At auditions the pin became a carefully planned prop: "Lest they think that I was making any effort, I used to get myself up in a sort of slouch costume. I had an old stocking cap . . . and an old green tweed coat. I would pin the coat together with a safety pin . . . I wanted to look as though it were really nothing to me if I got the part or didn't." Five years later she wore the coat and the pin in the film *Morning Glory* (1933), for which she won the Academy Award for best actress. When Hepburn showed up at the Parisian House of Balmain for a costume fitting for the stage production of *The Millionairess* (1952), the *directrice* looked askance at the actress's T-shirt sloppily pinned at the back of the neck to keep it from drooping.

"I've always had
a deep conviction
of my charms."
— Katharine Hepburn

"It never really

Hats became Hepburn's signature both on- and off-screen. During filming she kept sun hats handy, and at home, displayed them as mementoes of her favorite films. In *Woman of the Year*, she wore the loose-weave straw, top right. Opposite, Kate adds anklets and cork-wedge sandals for an impish touch to her trousers and flyaway shirt.

bothered me that people never considered me a beauty."

— Katharine Hepburn

In spite of public reaction, the simple safety pin had become Hepburn's signature.

Regardless of her apparent disregard for anything to do with trends or, worse, "current fashion," the cagey actress played the movie-star fashion role when she determined it was necessary. Before starting production on her first film, *Bill of Divorcement* in 1932, she demanded that director George Cukor, who would become her mentor, hire Coco Chanel to design an "appropriate" wardrobe, one of the first indications why she would be dubbed "Katharine of Arrogance." Cukor refused and assigned designer Josette De Lima. After the film, Hepburn and her then husband, Ludlow Ogden Smith (the pair divorced shortly thereafter), traveled to Paris, where she bought a Schiaparelli costume "on the chance that they would call me and tell me I was a hit." When Kate got the good news, she and Luddy exchanged their no-class tickets for first class, and the new star disembarked wearing the famed French couturiére's eggplant-colored three-quarter coat over a skirt and blouse, with a knitted hat. "Very easy to wear," she noted.

"We're all in a serious spot when the original bag lady wins a prize for the way she dresses."

— Katharine Hepburn

Although she was most often photographed in tennis shoes or sandals in the late thirties and forties, Kate turned to high heels when she wanted to be powerful. Script-writer Garson Kanin remembered her towering over Louis B. Mayer in "massively high heels" as she was trying to sell him *The Philadelphia Story* (1940) and attributed her success to those spikes. Others attributed it to the fact that she was having an affair with Howard Hughes, who had bought the film rights to the story for her immediately after she decided to do the play.

All this deliberate glamour earned Kate a place on New York's best-dressed list in 1940. Right in character, she was the only one of thirteen honorees who didn't show up at the Waldorf-Astoria to treat photographers to a day of puff pictures. Hepburn didn't want her public to think that she cared about such goings-on. The next year *McCall's* magazine named her its woman of the year, citing her beauty, grace, talent and devotion, as well as her "untraditional ways. She is a raving individual."

Individuality was a rarity in Hollywood. This gangly redhead with the less-than-feminine voice didn't wear makeup unless she was on camera, rolled her hair on homemade newspaper curlers (to

absorb the water quickly, a trick she still employs) and refused to eat in restaurants because the food upset her stomach and she didn't like people staring at her.

She always fought convention. In 1933 she bought a monkey and walked around with it perched on her shoulder. Gossip columnist Hedda Hopper wrote that Kate was, like Garbo, an "at-home nudist, presumably finding it better than air-conditioning for keeping her cool." But perhaps the most unconventional (and most controversial) aspect of Hepburn's life was her 30-year love affair with her famed co-star Spencer Tracy, a married Catholic. He hated her wardrobe, despised her trousers, laughed at her hats. When Tracy died in 1967, he left his beloved mistress a well-worn scarlet sweater, which she still wears when she's biking, and an old cap, which she lent to Henry Fonda to wear in *On Golden Pond* (1981).

By the time Tracy died, Kate had already begun to simplify her life. The process included simplifying her wardrobe decisions, paring her closet to the bare essentials: 20 pairs of neutral pants, white shirts from her favorite custom maker, Battaglia, and assorted solid-colored turtleneck and cardigan

A well-worn tweed blazer over a crew-neck Shetland sweater, this page, typifies Hepburn's fondness for combining textures. Note her hair, worn "a la concierge," her own creation that became her trademark. While scouting locations for *The Corn is Green* (1979), opposite, she tops her turtleneck and trousers with an oversized man's shirt.

K a t h a r i n e   H e p b u r n

Bold striped blouse is counter to Hepburn's subdued personal wardrobe in this studio coordinated publicity shot from the '40s. More glamorous publicity, opposite, Hepburn models a quilted coat ensemble, a feminized version of the smoking jacket.

"I'm very broad shouldered, long armed, like a gorilla."

— Katharine Hepburn

sweaters in white and black—and red, her favorite color. Hepburn rarely strayed from these pieces even at *haute*-fashion moments. Upon meeting Coco Chanel, whom she was portraying in the biographical Broadway musical *Coco*, Kate topped her casual uniform with a cap secured by a triangular scarf. (After giving the actress a very French once-over, Chanel's look implied, "I hope she can act.")

Indeed, Katharine Hepburn could act. She won four Academy Awards for her starring performances. Her consciously casual style has always been part of her performance: daring to act as though she didn't care how she looked, knowing all the while she was making a lasting impression. For that personal style Hepburn earned one of America's highest fashion honors at the age of 78. In 1985 the Council of Fashion Designers of America recognized the star with a lifetime achievement award, with Calvin Klein calling her "the epitome of style . . . everything that's modern." To accept her award she wore a black silk shirt, matching trousers and a long white scarf, an evening twist on her basic uniform.

Hepburn's was a rebellious, offhand chic in an era of studied, sexy glamour. Yet it is her emphasis on comfort and function mixed with panache that has prevailed as the basis for American sportswear. That she still wears layers of sweaters and turtlenecks with men's trousers is a credit to her earliest sense of style, tomboy style.

Lucile Ball

"I dislike anything excessive. It confuses me. I was happier when I had two dresses, both black."

— Lucille Ball

In the summer of 1946 the world *didn't* love Lucy. After significant research, MGM let Lucille Ball's movie contract lapse, not knowing how to market the talented comedienne with the Technicolor red hair. She lacked the sophistication of MGM's leading lady Katharine Hepburn and the sex appeal of Columbia's Rita Hayworth, even though she had been cast as a glamour girl for years. "I look like everybody's idea of an actress, but I feel like a housewife," Ball once observed. "I think that's what my trouble was in movies."

Instead of fighting her natural inclination, Lucy launched a television career and used her hausfrau heart to make comedic history. As a result, she has been the world's most beloved "housewife." Her wardrobe on the *I Love Lucy* show — season after season of frocks, dressmaker suits and capri pants — is the epitome of middle-America style in the 1950s. Although she wore designs inspired by Christian Dior's New Look of 1947, her often off-the-rack garb was a watered-down version of *haute couture*, understandable fashion for her female fans who whipped up Jell-O salads and tuna casseroles and then tuned in on Monday night.

Lucy's sense of style was bred in her acting school days, when, still a teenager, she supported herself by modeling for the famed designer Hattie Carnegie. Renowned for her elegant simplicity, Carnegie taught the struggling young actress how to dress, to stand and walk gracefully, and then pushed her out the door when Hollywood called in 1933. Scouts for Samuel Goldwyn Studios were in New York in search of a dozen glamorous photographer's models to rival Ziegfeld's showgirls. When they saw Lucy, a leggy bleached blonde (who coincidentally had a Chesterfield cigarette poster to her credit), they put her on a California-bound train the next day.

Once in Hollywood, the new troupe was evaluated by Goldwyn himself. Anxious to stand out in the gaggle of buxom beauties, a comedic Lucy used toilet tissue and stocking rolls to plump her contours. Her Chaplinesque humor was lost on the film mogul, who viewed her screen test and immediately rejected her. However, his trusted choreographer Busby Berkeley recognized her potential and

In one of her most glamorous photos, taken in the early '40s when studios were trying to shape her image as a leading lady, Lucille, the film actress, is dripping in diamonds and enveloped in tulle. Lucy's blond hair, opposite, was a short-lived phenomenon.

Lucille Ball

The many looks of
Lucy, from long-
lashed seductress,
this page, to fashion
plate, center, to
high-style yet
child-like clown.

"At heart, I'm a frustrated hairdresser."

— Lucille Ball

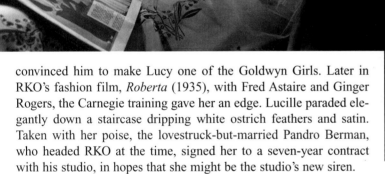

convinced him to make Lucy one of the Goldwyn Girls. Later in RKO's fashion film, *Roberta* (1935), with Fred Astaire and Ginger Rogers, the Carnegie training gave her an edge. Lucille paraded elegantly down a staircase dripping white ostrich feathers and satin. Taken with her poise, the lovestruck-but-married Pandro Berman, who headed RKO at the time, signed her to a seven-year contract with his studio, in hopes that she might be the studio's new siren.

In 1936 her model's body and elegant carriage showed off clothes so well that Hollywood stylists named Lucy the "Best-Dressed Girl in Town," an honor that may have made up for the fact that she wasn't beautiful by the prevailing Garbo/Dietrich standard. Her full face and bowed lips were in sharp contrast to the angular faces and simmering sex appeal of the glam girls of the day. Experts in the makeup department advised reshaping her brows, raising her hairline and capping her teeth to make her look chic, but nothing worked. Lucy wasn't destined to be RKO's siren.

The 29-year-old met 23-year-old Desi Arnaz when they were cast in the same film, *Too Many Girls* (1940). She was still in costume after a brawl scene and looked ravaged on their first meeting. At a party that night, Arnaz laid eyes on a refreshed Lucille Ball, a gorgeous blonde in beige pants and a form-fitting yellow sweater. Instantly enamored, they eloped in less than six months, on November 30, 1940. At her quickie wedding performed by a Connecticut justice of the peace, she sported a fox fur coat over a well-worn black dress. Nine years later the pair were married officially in a Catholic church, with Lucy decked out in a full-skirted blue satin dress and a clip-on white hat. At the time, not even she knew that the 1950s look she had chosen was a precursor to the *I Love Lucy* style that would establish her as a superstar.

"One day I saw a casting sheet that said 'a Lucille Ball type,' and that was the biggest thrill I ever had," Lucille noted about her days at RKO. But the thrill didn't last, she added: "I went into the casting office and

"Technicolor Tessie is a colorful girl."
— *Life Magazine*

told them I'd be available in a week, and they told me I was wrong for the part."

In 1942 slow box-office sales for her films forced RKO to find a competitor that would take over her contract. She landed at MGM, where studio designer Irene gave Lucy a newer, more glamorous image, a major change from the tailored dressmaker suits Edward Stevenson had designed at RKO. Irene instructed Lucy to gain ten pounds and wrapped her more voluptuous body in figure-revealing dresses and strapless gowns that bared her beautiful shoulders.

By now the young actress's curly mane had gone from bleached blonde to mousy brown. "There were enough blondes, so why not a redhead?" MGM studio stylist Sydney Guilaroff asked himself. Her strawberry-orange tresses became Lucy's signature, especially because the shade worked so well in Technicolor, the industry's new ultra-sensitive color film. Hedda Hopper claimed Lucy abhorred the hair color, quoting the young star, "I should wear a sign on my chest saying: I hate it, but Technicolor demands it." As time went on, her hair got brighter and brighter and eventually earned the moniker Tango Red. The carrot hue was so shocking, many cynics complained that no one had hair that color, to which Lucy curtly responded, "I do."

That strawberry-orange hair would be the only residual trapping of her glamour-girl days. After she left MGM, a failed leading lady, and began a successful career in radio, Lucy was free of makeup sittings and costume fittings and once again let her hair fade to natural brown. However, when Harry Cohn at Columbia put her under contract for films again, she went back to her Technicolor roots and kept them that way forever. A perfectionist about her hair, she had her own beauty salon at home. There she not only tended to her own color and style but to that of her friends. "There was a time I seriously considered becoming a hairdresser, but I didn't have enough money to take the course," the actress explained to the press. Columnist Louella Parsons pointed out that Lucy "loved hen parties. She's a great one for spending a Sunday giving her girlfriends home permanents."

While she was making comedies for Cohn, Lucy and Desi sold the *I Love Lucy* pilot to television. They were suddenly independent producers in a new industry, and Desilu eventually would become one of the most important television production companies in the history of Hollywood. As producers, they controlled everything about the show, including its fashion statement. The comedienne was comfortable playing the ditzy wife of a bandleader, wearing the same kind of clothing she might buy for herself in real life at stores such as

At home, Lucy dressed in soft shirt and trouser outfit, this page, probably to call the dog trainer. Note the Milk Bone dog biscuits on the counter. Behind the scenes of *The Lucy Show*, Ball relaxes in a jewel-encrusted caftan and can't resist wearing a cluster of carats on her ring finger, opposite.

"She has 10 closets filled with go out, she has nothing to wear."

— Desi Arnaz

Ohrbach's and The Broadway. After all, she had often said that her favorite clothes were casual. "Station wagon clothes, I call them — tweed suits and comfortable coats."

Far from being the ditz she played on the tube, Lucille the producer saw TV as the real-people medium. She felt her down-home approach to fashion might not be glamorous enough for films, but it was the perfect fit for the TV world. After a false start with costume designer Elois Jenssen, Lucy hired her former RKO designer Edward Stevenson to shape the prim and proper shirtwaist dresses and blouses with loose-fitting trousers that she wore in most scenes. When the script called for dress-up, Lucy donned taffeta cocktail gowns in which she purposely looked a bit uncomfortable, just the way Mrs. America felt when she went out on the town. Her strategy worked. Viewers not only adored Lucy, they went wild for her clothes. Dior's New Look dresses with their full skirts and fitted bodices became an American mainstay once women saw Lucy's little-screen adaptations. In the fall of 1952, some 2,800 retail stores offered consumers a full line of *I Love Lucy* dresses, sweaters, blouses and aprons. Thirty days after they went on the rack, more than 30,000 dresses and 32,000 aprons had been sold. Then came Desi smoking jackets and pajamas, which

sold out immediately. The Ricardos' wardrobe was a hit.

The Arnazes' marriage, however, was a definite miss. In March of 1960, America's most famous couple divorced, she claiming mental cruelty. Lucy wed her second husband, Gary Morton, in the fall of 1961, wearing the very same black-and-white suit that she had worn during the divorce proceedings. The next year Desi resigned as president of their Desilu production company, and Lucy took over. When she attended her first board of directors meeting as president, she was clad in a bright purple floral print dress. She had purposely dressed up for her new role. When Mr. Blackwell named her to his notorious Worst Dressed List, no one was surprised; the Lucy image was seriously out of date. She, after all, was still dressing for her best part — housewife — although the script had changed. Lucille had become a major Hollywood mogul.

Lucy Ricardo was Mrs. America with a funny bone and a fashion bent; the comedienne had worn the role well. But when *I Love Lucy* stopped production, she laid the fashion image to rest. Lucille Ball wanted simply "to look nice," as her daughter Lucie Arnaz puts it. Her heyday as a barometer of American fashion was over.

clothes, but every time we have to

A happy time at the Desilu ranch in California's San Fernando Valley, Desi Arnaz gets a hug from his love, Lucy. In her eyelet-trimmed frock, Lucille Ball confessed she was a homemaker at heart. That ideal set the tone for the Lucy Ricardo philosophy of dressing. Opposite, Lucille models black chiffon accented with diamond brooch at the waist.

Marilyn Monroe

The world's most legendary blonde made a point of talking about how uncomfortable she was wearing clothes, that she preferred to go without . . . and that, well, yes, when she dressed, she dressed for men. "They seem to understand me. . . ." And she, them.

Marilyn Monroe projected a profound rejection of the importance of clothing, a disregard for anything to do with fashion, and liked people to think she was totally oblivious to being a "sex symbol." But her insouciant attitude was all part of her carefully orchestrated image. In reality, Monroe was obsessed with how she looked and what she wore. She had to be. Making vulgar look guileless required absolute focus. Her unmade-bed look was her own creation — no designer took a hand in it until she had carefully defined its parameters. The rules were simple: Flaunt the body, tousle the hair, pout the lips.

Norma Jeane Baker, who spent most of her childhood in southern California foster homes and an orphanage, began manipulating her own image long before Hollywood found her and turned her into Marilyn Monroe. She learned to appreciate her God-given curves as an adolescent when she borrowed a too-tight sweater and wore it to school. To Norma Jeane's surprise, the boys ogled and four of them walked her home. Her body was suddenly her friend, she said, "a sort of magic friend." Fascinated with her new power, she spent much time between classes at Van Nuys High School in front of the mirror in the girls' bathroom, fiddling with her hair and cosmetics.

At 16 she married, went to work in a defense plant, and was discovered by a military photographer. She started modeling. Her first agent, Emmeline Snively, gets the credit for teaching Norma Jeane to lower her upper lip as she formed the perfect smile and that unexpected, quivering pout. She lost her first modeling assignment, however, because her body attracted more attention than the clothes. The round hips and dramatic breasts overpowered anything she put on. Photographers soon realized she was the perfect pinup. A career blossomed: model, cover girl, starlet.

Although she had several parts in the late 1940s, her minute-long strut in a Groucho Marx comedy called *Love Happy* (1950), coupled with a nude photo of her in a now-legendary calendar, brought the 24-year-old and her remarkable body to the public's eye. By the end of 1950 she had signed a six-month contract with 20th Century-Fox, right after her role in *All About Eve* (1950). By then, Norma Jeane was blonde, her teeth were straight, her nose reshaped and her name was Marilyn Monroe.

Convinced that her voluptuous body was her key to success, the driven actress found ways to use clothes to highlight each of her assets. In the postwar era of sexual repression, most women's skirts were well below their knees and their blouses had high collars, so Marilyn rebelled, showcasing her breasts, rear and thighs. Her strapless gowns, low-cut necklines, tight skirts and short-shorts were blatant. But on Marilyn, clinging turtleneck sweaters and snug slacks could achieve the same effect. All the while, her angelic face forced male fans to blame themselves for their lusty fantasies.

By 1953 her personal style was well honed and she was accepting

"In Hollywood a girl's virtue important than her hairdo."

— Marilyn Monroe

is much less

A fresh-faced Marilyn in the late '40s, opposite, was eagerly anticipating a movie career when she posed for this shot on a sunny California day. The young innocent developed into the ultimate glamour goddess complete with white-blond bouffant hair, cascading diamond earrings and the famed darkened mole, shown here on the night of John F. Kennedy's birthday party at Madison Square Garden.

At the premiere of *Gigi* (1958), beckoned by paparazzi, Monroe's character comes to life with her renowned quivering smile. "Marilyn" was a personality Norma Jeane Baker could turn off and on at will. Walking on a New York street with her friend Susan Strasberg, she asked "Hey, you want to see me be 'her'?" and immediately switched into her most famous role. Opposite, the star starts to apply her face in the Columbia makeup room. Note the bit of bare tummy peeking out under her midriff blouse.

"I like to be really dressed up or really undressed. I don't bother with anything in between."

— Marilyn Monroe

Photoplay magazine's prestigious "Fastest Rising Star" award. "When she wiggled through the audience to come up to the podium, her derriere looked like two puppies fighting under a silk sheet," writer James Bacon commented after the awards. He wasn't the only one who noticed. All Hollywood was talking about Marilyn's jiggling rear encased in the gold-lamé dress she had borrowed from the wardrobe of 1953's *Gentlemen Prefer Blondes.* Joan Crawford publicly called the young star a disgrace to the industry. Granted, Marilyn was sewn into the zipperless costume and resewn into it when seams split as she prepared to take the stage. But she knew exactly what she was doing. As Bacon's simile so succinctly pointed out, Marilyn's clothes brought out the innocence in raw sex, a trick she used forever.

Eschewing traditional undergarments was another way Marilyn delivered her dress-naked message. Because she had worked out with weights since her high school years, her breasts were firm enough to go braless, yet bouncy enough to seduce. The night in the early '60s when she wore a black eyelet gown to Peter Lawford's house, her nipples purportedly protruded through the little holes, dazzling all, especially her date, then U.S. Attorney General Robert Kennedy.

And because her shapely rear end was an intrinsic symbol of her sex appeal, panty lines were too distracting, so she simply eliminated them. When she was sewn into tight gowns, she instructed seamstresses to follow the curve of her butt, defining each cheek as best they could. The actress worked closely with designer Jean-Louis to create the flesh-toned, rhinestone-encrusted gown she wore to the celebration of President John F. Kennedy's 45th birthday at Madison Square Garden. She told him to "make this a dress that only Marilyn Monroe would dare to wear." The designer responded, "I take it you want this to be as nude as possible." As the spotlights went on, the $12,000 silk souffle mesh dress became virtually transparent, allowing her naked body to glisten as she sang "Happy Birthday" with an interlude personalized for the President to the tune of "Thanks for the Memory." The classic

"All those lines and ridges in they distort a girl, so I never wear them"

— Marilyn Monroe

undie-less Marilyn story occurred on a hot August day in New York when she, clad in a mink coat that husband Joe DiMaggio had given her, opened her fur to show a friend how she beat the heat — she was wearing nothing else.

Women all over the world took heed of Marilyn's fashion message: get sexier. Though her fans didn't go to her dress-naked extremes, the Hollywood goddess unintentionally started several trends. One of the first female superstars to be photographed in jeans, she had worn denims since her World War II job inspecting parachutes in a defense factory. She never gave them up, proving that even dungarees could look provocative. "Putting a girl in overalls is like having her work in tights, particularly if a girl knows how to wear them," she once said. She wore halter-neck dresses so frequently both on- and off-screen that the silhouette is still her fashion signature. Whether full-skirted or sheath, it emphasized the breasts, making them look larger. The low-cut, backless style meant that the dress itself provided the only support — again, no brassiere. Copies of the white halter-neck pleat-

ed dress she wore in *The Seven-Year Itch* (1955) became a hit in retail stores shortly after its premiere; versions are still available today. Her other trademark uniform came from Woolworth's, and she wore it well. Her bathrobe was a staple at home: she greeted guests in it, posed for portraits in it and was even interviewed by her biographers while wearing it. No one but Monroe could have convinced America that a simple white terry-cloth robe was an alluring alternative to a silk peignoir.

She used accessories as sensual tools of her trade and her fans saw them as cheap little ways to get the Monroe look. Her high-heeled clear-plastic platform sandals presented her bare feet like little gifts tied with changeable ribbons that matched her outfits. Marilyn was so attached to these shoes, she wore red ties for publicity photographs, white ties to match her two-piece swimsuit at home, and red again on the screen in *How to Marry a Millionaire* (1953). When plastic shoes weren't appropriate, Monroe picked the barest, strappiest leather sandals she could find and then went stockingless, for the clos-

undergarments are unnatural and

Joe DiMaggio loved to see Marilyn decked out in diamonds and furs, opposite, but hated her décolleté in public — her overexposure was one of the downfalls of their nine-month marriage. Her innocent over-the-shoulder glance was a natural pose when she first started her modeling career. Marilyn struck the same pose, right, thousands of times as she flirted with the camera and flaunted her derriere.

Marilyn often did her own makeup. Here, she's perched on a curb doing those lips, between scenes during *Clash by Night* (1952) at RKO Studios. When Marilyn got casual, opposite, she often opted for flats. The Italian shoemaker Ferragamo made dozens of pairs for her.

"I'm only comfortable when I'm naked"

— Marilyn Monroe

est thing to naked feet. After *How to Marry a Millionaire*, dangling diamond earrings became *de rigueur* (She rarely wore other jewelry for fear of detracting from her face and in fact gave away the emerald earrings that Frank Sinatra had given her).

If what she wore influenced fashion, her makeup and hair redefined beauty. Red lips, dark eyes, the painted mole. Hookers may have owned the look before, but Marilyn refreshed its appeal. A heavy makeup fan since she was a teen, she said she didn't understand its impact. "My arrival in school, with painted lips and darkened brows, started everyone buzzing. Why I was a siren, I hadn't the faintest idea. I didn't want to be kissed, and I didn't dream of being seduced by a duke or a movie star. The truth was that with all my lipstick and mascara and precocious curves, I was as unresponsive as a fossil. But I seemed to affect people quite otherwise." As she matured, however, she treasured her lips, knowing their seductive power. Making them look their fullest was a two-step process: three shades of lipstick blended together and coated with a glossy mixture of Vaseline petroleum jelly and wax. "The lipstick and the mascara were like clothes," she acknowledged. "They improved my looks as much as if I had put on a real gown."

Norma Jeane had been a successful model with golden brown hair, but Marilyn was born a bottle blonde. Though she evolved from her late '40s yellow-blonde to white blonde when she died in 1962, she kept

"If I'm going to be a symbol of something, I'd rather have it sex than some of the other things they've got symbols of."

— Marilyn Monroe

a shimmering beige for years. She even stayed out of the sun so her skin would remain the same shade as her hair, so nothing would take away from her features. At its lightest, "pillowcase white," her tousled mane was so pale that her roots had to be retouched every five days. Experts agreed that she looked more fragile and vulnerable as her hair color became more artificial.

What was demure for Monroe is cheap and trashy on her imitators, of which there have been many. In the more than thirty years since her death, Marilyn clones have copied her walk, her talk, her hair, her makeup, her wardrobe, even her smile. None have been able to capture her innocent demeanor. Not one has been able to trap two puppies fighting under a silk sheet.

something, I'd rather have it sex

After hours Monroe serenaded Hollywood columnist Sidney Skolsky in one of her famed halter-neck dresses. She wore a similar look, opposite far left, on-screen in *Niagara* (1952). When she divorced DiMaggio, opposite, she did it in style, but even her demure suit couldn't hide her sensuality.

Doris Day

Her famed freckles spelled innocence. Her buttercup blonde hair threatened no one. All-American Doris Day was always a trendsetter, several steps ahead of her fans, letting them know what was keen, cool or groovy, depending on the decade. She changed as fast as fashion, and her films evolved into two-hour style fests. Americans went to see her movies to learn how Doris Day got the guy and, just as important, to see what she wore when she got him.

In the early '50s when U.S. military men in Korea voted her "the girl we would most like to take a slow boat back to the U.S. with," she wore little dresses with white piqué collars, Bermuda shorts, sweaters and knee socks that were as sweet and innocently perky as her smile. Her image was as virginal as a young girl's should have been. Female fans quickly copied her casual, healthy style. They took to walking shorts with white shirts demurely tucked in; their favorite dress was shirtwaisted, full-skirted and neatly belted; and their lips were a pretty pink, just like their friend Doris's. Many darker-haired fans started thinking about going blonde. That's about the same time Clairol started suggesting that blondes indeed have more fun.

By 1959 Doris and her fans were maturing. She — and they — were bored with the sweet, virginal look. To boost her slipping box-office sales, she went through a fashion rite of passage. The girl next door got sexy and glamorous. Apple pie turned à la mode.

Doris Day devotees went crazy when they saw *Pillow Talk* (1959). She played a contemporary career girl who was as sexually repressed as they were, but, man, could she dress to give another message. Her high-fashion, sexy new wardrobes became her film signature from then on. Fans loved her dyed-to-match furs and chapeaux, her very modern dresses and curve-revealing suits. Everyone flipped over the spike heels with the pointed toes and the way her derriere pooched just enough to say "come hither," while she still looked indefatigably perky.

Doris's transition to fashion leader was in sync with her growth as a movie star. She already had established herself as her female fans' best friend; every woman in the audience related to her. She had shown American women how it was possible to be at once prim and ingenuously appealing in her earliest, sugary films, such as *Tea for Two* (1950), *On Moonlight Bay* (1951) and 1953's *Calamity Jane*, the film Doris still calls "the real me." Her best-selling records were as sweet as pie, songs to get moony-eyed over. Her girl-next-door image — which she openly abhorred and her husband-cum-agent Marty Melcher encouraged — had served her well.

A turning point in her career was her first dramatic character role, in *Love Me or Leave Me* (1955), in which she played torch singer Ruth Etting. She had a pithy part to demonstrate her talent, and her character was extremely sensual. For Doris, wearing seductive clothes and playing a lusty woman was like the first French kiss, a taste of passion. She responded and so did her audience. Her important roles in Alfred Hitchcock's *The Man Who Knew Too Much* (1956) and the musical *The Pajama Game* (1957) confirmed her capabilities as an actress.

are provocative. . . "

— Doris Day

Doris may have worn every-girl clothes so her fans would relate, but, on page 98, the cluster of diamonds on her finger proved that she was living a movie-star life. You can almost hear the giggles as she posed in her pedal pushers, opposite. She was more sophisticated in capris, left, and a hoot in her sweatsuit.

In *Pillow Talk*, Doris found her success formula: subtly erotic comedy and great clothes. The peppy blonde gave millions of American women the courage to pull out all the stops when it came to being alluring. She taught women by example that sex was officially OK. In her various parts as the '60s career woman, this role model flaunted her figure and her beauty, infusing her characters with sexual energy. She wore backless gowns that brought attention to her voluptuous rear. Instead of using adhesive tape to minimize her very large bosom, she began emphasizing her provocative

In her Warner Brothers days, studio executives glamorized Day in *Romance on the High Seas* (1948), but she found her best glamour look off screen, center, when she attended the 1959 Academy Awards. Costume designers agreed with James Garner, so they played up her curvaceous figure, right.

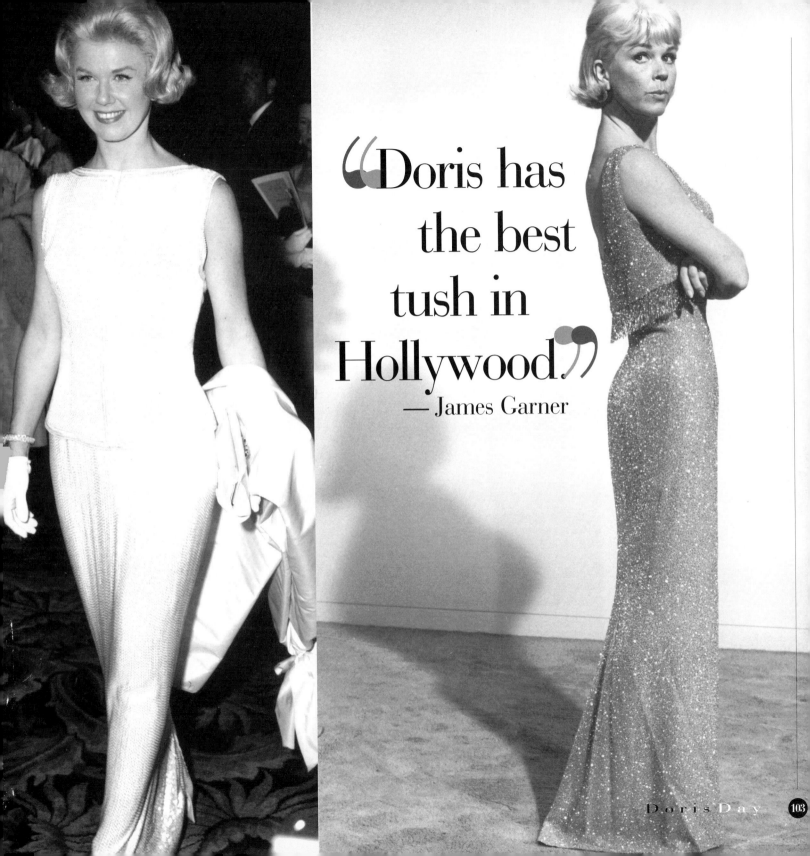

"Doris has the best tush in Hollywood."
— James Garner

"I knew Doris Day before she was a virgin"

— Oscar Levant

Describing the universal appeal of his co-star in *It Happened to Jane* (1959), Jack Lemmon compared Doris's power to the other blonde of the day. Doris, he said, had "an enticing sexual quality that is there but subliminal. She doesn't lay it out there like a Marilyn Monroe, but it's there nevertheless — the difference between a nude and a woman in seductive clothing." Ironically, a few years later Day would replace Monroe in *Something's Got to Give*, and the film was retitled *Move Over, Darling* (1963). The scene in which Marilyn swam in the nude was rewritten. Instead, Doris accidentally got drenched in a carwash, while wearing a dressmaker suit.

Producer Ross Hunter, who had ordered her image overhaul for *Pillow Talk*, was the first to realize that the sunny-faced actress was a trendsetter. Budgets for her wardrobe expanded; designers such as Irene, Jean-Louis and Ray Aghayan took turns dressing her. By the mid '60s Doris herself became

curves. Her Dutch-Boy bobs became lacquered, high-fashion coiffures, the bouffant that became the trend in American beauty salons.

Her career skyrocketed. In 1959 Hedda Hopper's readers voted Doris the number-one female star of the year, and from 1960 to 1965 she was queen bee at the American box office. The sexy Miss Day was on top.

fanatical about what she wore and how she looked on screen. She insisted on meticulous fittings that often lasted seven to nine hours, each ensemble requiring revision after revision. And although she cautioned her fans not to "dress for the sake of fashion," and said that trends meant nothing to her ("I don't care if *Vogue* approves," she once wrote), in those days she followed every new fad. Often she

The Dutch bob, Doris's favorite off-screen hair style, suits her nautical separates in *Glass Bottom Boat* (1966). Designer Ray Aghayan captured her outdoorsy spirit, but the following year had the challenge of turning her into a mod in *Caprice* (1967). The wardrobe test photo, opposite, shows the wide range of new looks Doris demanded for the film.

AIR FORCE

Today's devoted animal rights advocate blushes knowing that she once wore furs both on-screen and off, and isn't that an alligator hatbox? In a bathrobe-style coat, opposite, Doris arrives at the studio ready for hair and makeup. Note her cork wedgies.

I can't

wear anything too high-styled.”

— Doris Day

styled herself like a blonde Jacqueline Kennedy, complete with bouffant flip. Other times she went for street fashion. Aghayan remembers having to redesign her *Caprice* wardrobe three times, with the 42-year-old actress demanding that the clothes look younger, like those she had seen on the mods in London. Aghayan says he dressed her in the shortest skirts on the screen at the time, all grazing the knees.

She preferred her new high-fashion image to the "glamorous" one that Warner Brothers had foisted upon her in the late '40s and early '50s. Back then, when the studio's executives and stylists tried to glamorize her, she balked but did as she was told. "Name any picture I made for Warners and I will show you Doris Day in a ludicrous costume," she once said about those early glamour girl days. "Off-the-shoulder dresses with heart-shaped necklines, satin stoles that slid off my neck at the wrong times, flounces and frills and Barbie Doll crinolines. I would see myself on the screen and go home and cry all night." Until her name spelled big bucks at the box office, however, she didn't have much pull. If director Michael Curtiz, who had given Doris her first part in *Romance on the High Seas* (1948), wanted her in a long blond wig à la Bacall or with curls piled high like Crawford, that's what she wore. If keeping a part meant wearing a spangled dress, she grimaced and put it on. "I've always worn my hair in a Dutch bob," explained Day, née Doris von Kappelhoff, the daughter of a music teacher and his wife who sepa-

"I had become a new kind of sex go to bed with, but

rated when she was 12. "But there I was on the screen, a pancaked, lacquered Hollywood purse made out of a Cincinnati sow's ear." During her contract years with Warner (1948-1955) Doris's popularity expanded her power and her fashion confidence grew. She started dressing in the perkiest, crispest and most decidedly contemporary

costumes that the script would allow. She pursued a clean-cut image. "One thing I was careful about in my films was to avoid vulgarity, which I despise."

Though she made certain she was a trendsetter on screen, Doris's off-screen garb still looked more like Miss American Pie than the *tarte tatin* she had become in her films. In the '60s and '70s she could been seen riding her bike through the streets of Beverly Hills wearing her Bermudas and coordinated sweaters. Now she favors very tailored clothes, especially slacks, but will don a midi-length skirt and boots for day. And, of course, as a longtime animal rights advocate, she never wears fur coats. "When I think back, I could die that I wore furs," she declares. But, as she later acknowledged, "it was so easy to fall into a celebrity trap and start living up to the expected image." For Hollywood galas she often simply turned to her costume closet.

Doris kept just about every costume from her fashion films and guarded them as carefully as she did her image. In fact, when Irene was nominated for an Academy Award for her *Midnight Lace* (1960) designs, she wanted to borrow back one coat and Doris resisted until the famed designer promised to return it the next day.

When the star and husband Marty Melcher separated in 1961, he

symbol—the woman men want to not until they marry her" — Doris Day

It's easy to see that the diamonds are real on Doris's neck and ears, while those sparkles on her gown are just cut glass. She hated this lacquered upswept do that the Warner Brothers hairdresser concocted. The bugle-beaded midriff top and shorts helped spark this cheesecake photo, opposite.

"She has thin, well-proportioned enormous bust —

Doris tried her hand at designing clothes that her fans could buy. She captured her own innocence in this floral sundress and coordinating sweater. In the '60s Doris's satin ensemble was as bouffant as her hair, opposite.

legs, a small waist and an the biggest shock, because who ever knew she had it?"

— Ms. Magazine, January 1976

came back bearing a diamond ring of more than four carats as a symbol of his love. Doris couldn't help but notice that the stone "had a flaw in it big enough to see with the naked eye," and although they got together again, their relationship was also flawed. She said she had lost her feeling for him and that there would be no sex; they had separate bedrooms. She was getting all the loving she needed on-screen, in her fan mail.

Her fashion fanaticism paid off. Fans have been faithful for years. Though Doris Day hasn't made a film since 1968, the loyal still report on her wardrobe, as in this excerpt from a newsletter written by her fan-club president Michael V. Doyle in early 1990, more than 40 years after her Hollywood film debut:

Just so you can picture our dear "Calamity Jane," I'll give you a session-by-session outline of her attire!! On Friday she was in cream from head to toe with a lovely, soft, long skirt and jacket, a turtleneck sweater, boots and pearls. My favorite outfit came next — on Saturday morning. She had on a long medium-blue denim skirt, brown boots and belt, white turtleneck and red-and-white checked blouse — a real "Doris Day look"! At Saturday night's banquet she was wearing a tailored black suit, white blouse with black polka dots and boots, and then on Sunday morning she wore brown flat shoes and a fun cream-colored pants outfit that had the cut of a pretty jogging suit. Her hair is about an inch below her ears, and the style is a somewhat tousled page-boy with bangs. It looked great!

AuDrey Hepburn

Scrawny hardly described a glamour girl in the '50s heyday of Marilyn Monroe and Elizabeth Taylor. Nor were a flat chest and bushy eyebrows the attributes of a "movie star." Then along came Audrey Hepburn, a ballerina flung into a hoofer's world, an ingenue among the postwar sex goddesses. Ugly duckling redux.

Actually, the 98-pound waif wasn't as guileless as her doe eyes suggested to the world. Determined to be a fashion icon (and forever denying that she was one), her image was as calculated as other stars' and carefully conceived to be uniquely hers. She knew exactly what worked and how to use it. When the glam girls went for décolletage, she elected the turtleneck; her presumed innocence was more powerful than the biggest breasts.

"I always looked like such a good little girl, and I always used that image to my advantage," Audrey admitted. She was reflecting on her World War II childhood in the Netherlands when, serving as a messenger for the Resistance and confronted by Nazi soldiers, she feigned naivete long enough to charm her potential captors with her innocent eyes and a handful of daisies. However, that same formula worked as she tiptoed onto the Hollywood scene and made off with stardom her first time out, in *Roman Holiday* (1953).

When Edith Head, the renowned costume designer assigned to the picture, took a first look, she thought Audrey's neck too long, her shoulders too wide, brows too bold, teeth too crooked and feet too big. She immediately prescribed falsies. "What are those?" the demure Belgian-born starlet asked before rejecting the faux curves.

"No, thank you," too, to caps for her teeth. And no, not a single hair was to be plucked from the eyebrows.

Once she understood the ground rules, Head regrouped and reassessed the offbeat beauty. "She was a girl ahead of fashion, who deliberately looked different from other women, who dramatized her slenderness into her chief asset," the designer later reflected. Their ten-hour fittings turned into a Hollywood conspiracy, an attack on the meaning of allure, a new and very carefree approach to beauty.

Every decision was made with the intention of amplifying the real Audrey, not hiding her then-unfashionable figure: extra design details to further define those bony shoulders, collars designed to actually accentuate the length of the swanlike neck, no pads to round her narrow hips. Together Head and Hepburn took advantage of her lithe dancer's body. The star took to actually sketching costumes on "little Audreys" (Head's pre-printed sketch pads bearing Hepburn's figure and face) to show the designer what she wanted. Every machination led the disarmed viewer hopelessly to that face. The audience was hers.

But Hepburn quickly outgrew the conservative Head's designs. In her 1954 film *Sabrina*, Hepburn's character would undergo a fashion transformation; so too would Audrey. Afraid to let Head handle *Sabrina* alone, Hepburn headed to France to pursue French couture designers for the film. Her first choice, Cristobal Balenciaga, then one of the biggest names in Parisian fashion, turned down the oppor-

Not really as shapeless as her legend portrays, Hepburn had a dancer's body, with strong thighs and a well-defined derriere. She shows off a tiny waist by criss-crossing the tails of a man's shirt and knotting them at the back.

"By any beauty parlor or beauty contest standard she is hopelessly ill-proportioned and unsymmetrical."

— *Photoplay,* 1957

tunity to dress this unconventional young star. Next on her list was the upstart Hubert de Givenchy, who actually was expecting to meet Katharine when a Hepburn appeared on his appointment list. Charmed by Audrey at their first encounter, Givenchy would become her lifelong friend and image collaborator. He understood Hepburn's insecurities about her imperfections. He realized that her emaciation was self-imposed, a remnant of a war-torn childhood when she was forced into hiding from the Nazis and used mind control to avoid starvation while surviving on tulip bulb grist and rainwater. He knew, too, that hers was a mannequin's figure, born to display fashion. Givenchy created clothes that celebrated that boyish body. Audrey had already used it to survive; now it would be her ticket to becoming a fashion legend.

At Hepburn's insistence, Head used many of Givenchy's designs in *Sabrina,* but the French couturier got no screen credit and, in fact, Head won an Academy Award for their combined efforts. But Givenchy won the real prize. After the success of *Sabrina,* Audrey's new husband, Mel Ferrer, encouraged her to create a trademark look on- and off-screen. Those signature styles would come from her work with Givenchy. She would be his muse and he her designer for the next 40 years. "She was terribly insecure about her bustline," recalled the French designer. "But I told her people would look at her eyes first, no matter what size her breasts were."

Off-screen she sought refuge in the comfort of his clothes. "Givenchy outfits gave me 'protection' against strange situations and people because I felt so good in them," she confessed. The pair worked together in Paris, shaping what would come to be known as the Audrey Hepburn look: always the finest fabrics, slim sheaths, bare necklines that exposed her clavicles or perfect collars that hugged her neck, full skirts to visually whittle her tiny 20-inch waist, triangular scarfs tied bandanna style under her chin, those oversized sunglasses. And, of course, the black bateau-necked Sabrina dress that showed up in department store windows and on American women just weeks after the film made its debut.

Hepburn was so ahead of fashion in the late '50s that even ultra-style-conscious First Lady-to-be Jacqueline Kennedy elected to wear the Audrey Hepburn look — especially pill-box hats and streamlined suits — during her husband's campaign. The look was so elegant that both women would eventually become doyennes of classic style.

No matter how much credit she gave to Givenchy for "creating" her in the four decades following their meeting in 1953, Hepburn's image was her own doing. In her personal wardrobe she was fastidious, controlling and always creative. *She* stripped away distracting accessories to keep herself unadorned like a fine piece of sculpture. *She* donned the black bodysuit that made shapeless a desirable body type. *She* neglected to button the men's shirts she wore as a uniform, wrapping and cinching the shirttails around her waist to turn a little-boy look into a statement of chic. *She* chose to wear her sweaters backwards. *She* determined that 5'6¾" was tall enough, eschewing cumbersome stiletto heels for ballet slippers and flats. *She* knew what worked for

"Some people dream of having

a big swimming pool — with me, it's closets. "

— Audrey Hepburn

At a real Tiffany event, opposite, Audrey elects to wear a major diamond fantasy. In 1958, the star was named to New York's list of the "Ten Best-Dressed Women" for the second consecutive year. Center, the green velvet chemise over a floor-length hobble skirt by Hubert de Givenchy was one of her favorite gowns. On the golf course, the barefoot ingenue strikes an impish pose in a white sundress.

"I didn't hide anything of hers. I let her be."

— Hubert de Givenchy

Hepburn, what beguiled and enhanced.

Sometimes her principles of style conflicted with the technical side of making movies. In *Funny Face* (1957) director Stanley Donen insisted she wear white socks with otherwise all-black dancer's garb, very much like her off-screen uniform, lest she fade into the background. To his surprise, the young actress protested vehemently that the stockings would break the continuous all-black line that made legs look longer. When he couldn't be swayed, Hepburn threw a tearful fit and disappeared to her dressing room, only to return to the set a few minutes later, defeated but composed, ready to continue in clean white socks. After she saw the scene on the screen, Audrey sent Donen a thank-you note acknowledging, "You were right about the socks."

Despite her innate fashion sense, when directors occasionally rejected Givenchy for a Hepburn film, she got nervous. During the filming of *Two for the Road* (1967) Stanley Donen nixed Givenchy in favor of off-the-rack designs à la Paco Rabanne and Mary Quant. Hepburn fought over every detail, determined to preserve her carefully cultivated image. At least one cos-

tume designer quit, and Hepburn refused more than 75 garments in search of the final 23 she wore on screen. When the film hit the screen, she was sporting a totally new look: clinging jersey mini dresses in frenetic stripes and vibrant colors. Audiences looked beyond the mod '60s clothes, saw elegant Audrey validating a young trend, and felt liberated to expand their own fashion parameters. But more than that, she was opening the door for sophisticated women to appreciate fashion that came from the streets rather than the runways.

When he cast her in *They All Laughed* (1981), director Peter Bogdanovich was canny enough to appreciate Hepburn's casual pea-coat-and-jeans off-screen style, so he personally selected her entire film wardrobe from her closet.

Even her on-screen makeup was dictated by her everyday look, a style that mesmerized photographer Cecil Beaton, who eventually became her costume designer for *My Fair Lady* (1964) and observed her work from her earliest days in Hollywood. "She wears no powder, so that her white skin has a bright sheen. Using a stick of greasepaint with a definite stroke, she draws

The red Givenchy coat, opposite, from *Charade* (1964) became part of Hepburn's personal wardrobe. "I wore it until the threads began to separate and it was shiny on the edges." Givenchy went to a creative extreme with this leopard-skin toque. In her teens, this page, Hepburn's lean form drew a variety of responses, as she modeled at tea time.

This page, clad in the Givenchy pillbox-and-suit style that Jackie Kennedy adapted, Hepburn sits with her pup, Famous. Opposite, Hepburn's off-screen uniform with its slightly raised bateau neckline makes her long neck look shorter.

"She may singlehandedly make bazooms a thing of the past."
— Billy Wilder

heavy bars of black upon her naturally full brows and, almost in Fratellini fashion, liberally smudges both upper and lower lids with black. To complete the clown boldness, she enlarges her mouth even at the ends." The makeup magic Beaton described would be copied by big-eyed models throughout the 1960s. But Audrey had created the look for herself simply because, after thoroughly evaluating her own look, she concluded that this was the only makeup that fully suited her, that didn't look as if she were trying to hide.

Unlike her Hollywood contemporaries, Hepburn aged with a grace relatively unknown in the film world. Rather than clinging to the image that had made her a star, she let herself evolve, honoring her comfort over trends, fads and her past. "Don't fight with your past image," she would offer as beauty advice. When the ingenue face was gone, so were the bangs, the heavy eyeliner, the bold brows. Instead she opted for less rather than more makeup, letting her hazel eyes speak softly for themselves. Though she had been faithful to a neutral-toned wardrobe as a young girl, she opted for more color as she aged. Vibrant red, warm peach, bright pink clothing cast a gentle glow on her skin and didn't necessitate harsh blushing powders and dark lipsticks.

Always the woman of quiet grace with a dancer's carriage that was as integral to her look as her sunglasses and lean limbs, Hepburn surrounded herself with calm. When stardom got too hectic, she retreated to her family and the peace of her beloved Switzerland. If she was on location with a film for prolonged periods of time, she would bring furniture from home or order white slipcovers for every piece of existing furniture. From a suitcase filled with her own accessories, she created her special, familiar environment to escape the chaos wherever she was. At home in her Swiss villa, *La Paisible*, "the peaceful place," she relished and nurtured her flower and vegetable gardens. There, too, she nurtured what mattered most to her, the relationships she enjoyed with her beloved sons, Sean and Luca. Over the course of her lifetime Hepburn was married to two very different men, Ferrer and Andrea Dotti, and lived her last years in the company of Robert Wolders, her love of 10 years.

Audrey Hepburn tightly controlled the world of Audrey Hepburn. It was the way she wanted it to be. She prioritized her life carefully: family first, her image and career next. She controlled the first in total privacy. The public Audrey, with her carefully cultivated style, was for the world to adore.

Epilogue

Each of these Hollywood women had a carefully scripted role in life, one she wrote, cast and directed. They all achieved boffo notices and they all were occasionally panned. That's the thing about personal style. Nobody likes every aspect of someone else's.

Although the clothes and the diamonds and the gloves and the shoes and the makeup added up to what we saw, none of those determined the icon status of our ten leading ladies. Call it inner beauty, call it star quality, call it image confidence — they all had it. If they didn't, when they came to Hollywood, they determinedly found it and hung on to it forever. It wasn't just that they could paint a fine face or swath a gorgeous body. First, they had carriage. Each knew how to handle her body to suit her image. Just as Audrey Hepburn walked as if a string attached her head to heaven as she glided through life, Marilyn Monroe wiggled into stardom and Joan Crawford swung her shoulders to the top. They knew that body image communicated at least half their message. Their presence was always acknowledged. Second, they trusted their own judgment. They didn't always do as they were told. And, in so doing, they always seemed to create trends rather than follow them.

We can learn from these ten legends. Nobody needs Dolores Del Rio's money, Katharine Hepburn's education or Doris Day's freckles to have a definite, individual image. The key word is individual. As Pirandello says, "a person has style who has things of his own to say and knows how to say them in his own way." Each of us needs to peer into our closets, pull out our favorite pieces, combine them in our favorite way, and find our personal style. For most of us, style is a discovery and is found through observation, creativity and trial and error. But it *is* within each of us, and within our closets — we just have to look. Our Hollywood fashion icons found theirs. We can too.

Researching the style of Hollywood legends requires the input of many people who themselves are special stars. I wish to thank everyone who shared their thoughts, their work and most especially their time and care.

Without the enthusiastic and tireless support of Stacey Behlmer of the Academy of Motion Picture Arts & Sciences' Center for Motion Picture Study Margaret Herrick Library, *Star Style* would never have evolved to what it is. Her knowledge added greatly to this work and I will remain forever grateful.

My gratitude, too, to the families, friends and co-workers of the legendary stars: Carol Eyerman, Raymond Daum, Douglas Whitney, Bob Schiffer, Sydney Guilaroff, Bob Mackie, Ray Aghayan, Marjorie Plecher Snyder, Ross Hunter, Stanley Donen, Lupita Tovar Kohner, Lucie Arnaz, Onna White, Gloria Daly, Joe Jasgur; especially to Roz Rogers and her very dear husband, Henry, who were so important to this project.

In the process, help comes in many different shapes and forms. I thank all of the following people for theirs: Bob and Susan Davis, Jessica Davis, Neil Davis, Effie Blackburn, Katie Cohn, Anne Ready, Lloyd Hassencahl, Deborah Durham, Jacqueline Balliu, Bruce Cohn Curtis, Leonard Finger, Kendall Carly Browne, Devery Freeman, Bijou Durden, Wilfrid Daly, Lou Valentino, Jeanne Buiter, Ann Calistro, Neil Feineman, Ellen Hoffs, Judy Hilsinger, Sandy Mendelson, Jennifer Nelson, Rebecca Austin, Laura Dail, Laura Perry, Marc Wanamaker, George Marcelle, Carlos Lamboy, David and Genevieve McAuley, Greg Schreiner, the dedicated members of Marilyn Remembered, Patrick Miller, Betty Goodwin, Harris Shepard, Cri Cri Solak-Eastin, Sylvia Sheppard, Tiffany & Company's Annamarie V. Sandecki, Ernie Lehman, Rudy Behlmer; Linda Mehr, Franz Offermans, Dan

Acknowledgments

Woodruff and the photography department of the Academy of Motion Picture Arts & Sciences' Center for Motion Picture Study; Adele Yellin, Fred Hayman, Jan Brilliot, Sandy Ryan, Deborrah Langbehn, Vera Brown, Wayne Massarelli, Harvey Rosenbloom, Laura Wenke and Sam and Sylvia Schulman.

Publishers are the first to confirm that a book is worthy of the public. For their confidence, I am grateful to the angels at Angel City Press: my creative editor Jean Penn, as well as Scott McAuley and Paddy Calistro. Also to Andrea Dovichi, for her positive attitude and hard work.

This book is beautiful not just because of the gorgeous women whose style it records, and not just because of the hundreds of unsung photographers whose pictures have become a part of motion picture history, but also because of its talented designer John Miller. John's eye for the unusual and his love of Hollywood captured the essence of each star. He translated it all into a visually beautiful gift.

My fondest thanks to Bob Cohn, Dick and Marian King and Amir Kojoory for their constant flow of ideas, concern and enthusiasm for *Star Style*. And finally, to my parents for their everlasting love.

—Patty Fox, Beverly Hills, 1995

Bibliography

Patrick Agan, *Is That Who I Think It Is?*, Ace Books, A Grosset & Dunlap Company, New York, 1976

Steven Bach, *Marlene Dietrich: Life and Legend*, William Morrow, New York, 1992

Kathleen Brady, *Lucille: The Life of Lucille Ball*, Hyperion, New York, 1994

Andrew Britton, *Katharine Hepburn: The Thirties and After*, Tyneside Cinema, Great Britain, 1984

Jim Brochu, *Lucy in the Afternoon*, William Morrow & Co., New York, 1990

Sven Broman, *Conversations with Greta Garbo*, Viking, New York, 1991

John Bryson, *The Private World of Katharine Hepburn*, Little Brown and Company, Boston/Toronto/London, 1990

James Card, *Seductive Cinema*, Alfred A. Knopf, New York, 1994

Larry Carr, *Four Fabulous Faces*, Galahad Books, New York, 1970

Larry Carr, *More Fabulous Faces*, Doubleday & Co., Inc., New York, 1979

Joel Cohen, *Laugh with Lucy*, Scholastic Book Services, New York, 1974

Christina Crawford, *Mommie Dearest*, William Morrow, New York, 1978

Joan Crawford, *My Way of Life*, Simon & Schuster, New York, 1971

Raymond Daum, *Walking With Garbo*, HarperCollins, New York, 1991

Daphne Davis, *Stars*, Stewart, Tabori & Chang, New York, 1983

Marlene Dietrich, *Marlene*, Grove Press, New York, 1987

Marlene Dietrich, *Marlene Dietrich's ABC*, Doubleday & Co., Inc. New York, 1962

Susan Doll, *Marilyn: Her Life & Legend*, Publications International Ltd., Illinois, 1990

Anne Edwards, *A Remarkable Woman*, William Morrow & Co., New York, 1985

Michael Freedland, *Katharine Hepburn*, W.H. Allen, London, 1984

Alan Gelb, *The Doris Day Scrapbook*, Grosset & Dunlap, New York, 1977

Richard Griffith, *The Movie Stars*, Doubleday & Co., New York, 1970

Boze Hadleigh, *Hollywood BabbleOn*, A Birch Lane Press Book, Published by Carol Publishing Group, 1994

Edith Head and Jane Kesner Ardmore, *The Dress Doctor*, Little Brown & Company, Boston, Toronto, 1959

Edith Head and Paddy Calistro, *Edith Head's Hollywood*, E.P. Dutton, New York, 1983

Katharine Hepburn, *ME*, Alfred A. Knopf, New York, 1992

Charles Higham, *Kate*, Norton & Co., New York, 1975

Charles Higham, *Lucy: The Real Life of Lucille Ball*, St. Martin's Press, New York, 1986

David Hofstede, *Audrey Hepburn: A Bio-Bibliography*, Greenwood Press, Connecticut/London, 1994

Hedda Hopper, *The Whole Truth and Nothing But*, Doubleday, New York, 1963

A.E. Hotchner, *Doris Day: Her Own Story*, William Morrow & Co., New York, 1976

Richard Hudson & Raymond Lee, *Gloria Swanson*, Castle Books, New York, 1970

Tom Hutchinson, *Screen Goddesses*, Exeter Books, New York, 1984

Caroline Latham, *Audrey Hepburn*, Proteus Publishing, New York/London, 1984

Caroline Latham, *Katharine Hepburn: Her Film & Stage Career*, Proteus Books, London/New York, 1982

Don Macpherson and Louise Brody, *Leading Ladies*, St. Martin's Press, New York, 1986

George Masters, *The Masters Way to Beauty*, E.P. Dutton, New York, 1977

Diana Maychick, *Audrey Hepburn*, Birch Lane Press, New York, 1984

Berniece Baker Miracle and Mona Rae Miracle, *My Sister Marilyn*, Algonquin Books of Chapel Hill, 1994

Marilyn Monroe, *My Story*, Stein and Day, New York, 1974

Ethan Mordden, *Movie Star*, St. Martin's Press, New York, 1983

Sheridan Morley, *Audrey Hepburn: A Celebration*, Pavilion Books, New York, 1993

George Morris, *Doris Day*, Pyramid Books, New York, 1976

Roy Newquist, *Conversations with Joan Crawford*, The Citadel Press, New Jersey, 1980

Barry Paris, *Garbo*, Alfred A. Knopf, New York, 1995

James Robert Parish, *The Hollywood Beauties*, Arlington House Publishers, New York, 1978

Lawrence J. Quirk, *The Films of Joan Crawford*, The Citadel Press, New Jersey, 1968

Lawrence J. Quirk, *The Films of Gloria Swanson*, The Citadel Press, New Jersey, 1984

Anna Raeburn, *Legend: Joan Crawford*, Little Brown & Co., Boston/Toronto, 1986

Randall Riese and Neal Hitchens, *The Unabridged Marilyn: Her Life from A to Z*, Congdon & Week, Inc., New York/Chicago, 1987

Maria Riva, *Marlene Dietrich*, Alfred A. Knopf, New York, 1993

Henry Rogers, *Walking The Tightrope*, William Morrow & Co., New York, 1980

Helen Rose, *Just Make Them Beautiful*, Dennis-Landman Publishers, Santa Monica, 1976

Helen Rose, *The Glamorous World of Helen Rose*, Rubidoux Printing, Riverside, California, 1983

Jeannie Sakol, photos by Joseph Jasgur, *The Birth of Marilyn*, St. Martin's Press, New York, 1991

Schirmer/Mosel, *Portraits, Marlene Dietrich 1926-1960*, Grove, Munich, 1984

Sam Shaw, *The Joy of Marilyn*, Exeter Books, New York, 1979

David Shipman, *Movie Talk*, St. Martin's Press, New York, 1988

James Spada, *Hepburn: Her Life in Pictures*, Doubleday & Co., New York, 1993

Gloria Swanson, *Swanson on Swanson*, Random House, New York, 1980

Lauren Tarshis, *Kate: The Katharine Hepburn Album,* Perigee, New York, 1993

Bob Thomas, *Joan Crawford*, Simon & Schuster, New York, 1978

Paul Trent, *The Image Makers*, Bonanza Books, New York, 1982

Alexander Walker, *Audrey Hepburn: Her Real Story*, St. Martin's Press, New York, 1994

Christopher Young, *The Films of Doris Day*, The Citadel Press, New Jersey, 1977

Index

Index

Photo Credits